THE DESIGNS OF
DONALD A. GARDNER

130 Best-Selling Home Plans

HOME PLANNERS

THE DESIGNS OF
DONALD A. GARDNER

Published by Home Planners, LLC
Wholly owned by Hanley-Wood, LLC

President, Jayne Fenton
Chief Financial Officer, Joe Carroll
Vice President, Publishing, Jennifer Pearce
Vice President, Retail Sales, Chuck Tripp
Vice President, General Manager, Marc Wheeler
Executive Editor, Linda Bellamy
National Sales Manager, Book Division, Julie Marshall
Managing Editor, Jason D. Vaughan
Special Projects Editor, Kristin Schneidler
Associate Editors, Nate Ewell, Kathryn R. Sears
Lead Plans Associate, Morenci C. Clark
Plans Associates, Jill M. Hall, Elizabeth Landry, Nick Nieskes
Proofreaders, Douglas Jenness, Sarah Lyons
Technical Specialist, Jay C. Walsh
Lead Data Coordinator, Fran Altemose
Data Coordinators, Misty Boler, Melissa Siewert
Production Director, Sara Lisa
Production Manager, Brenda McClary

Big Designs, Inc.
President, Creative Director, Anthony D'Elia
Vice President, Business Manager, Megan D'Elia
Vice President, Design Director, Chris Bonavita
Editorial Director, John Roach
Assistant Editor, Tricia Starkey
Director of Design and Production, Stephen Reinfurt
Group Art Director, Kevin Limongelli
Photo Editor, Christine DiVuolo
Art Director, Jessica Hagenbuch
Graphic Designer, Mary Ellen Mulshine
Graphic Designer, Lindsey O'Neill-Myers
Assistant Photo Editor, Mark Storch
Project Director, David Barbella
Assistant Production Manager, Rich Fuentes

Photo Credits

Front Cover: Design HPT910001; for details see page 16.
©1999 Donald A. Gardner, Inc, Photography courtesy of Donald A. Gardner Architects, Inc.

Back Cover: Design HPT910051; for details see page 96.
©1994 Donald A. Gardner Architects, Inc, Photography courtesy of Donald A. Gardner Architects, Inc.

Home Planners Corporate Headquarters
3275 W. Ina Road, Suite 220
Tucson, Arizona 85741

Distribution Center
29333 Lorie Lane
Wixom, Michigan 48393

© 2003

10 9 8 7 6 5 4 3 2 1

Printed in the United States of America

Library of Congress Control Number: 2003105314

ISBN softcover: 1-931131-18X

Design HPT910075, page 124

THE DESIGNS OF
DONALD A. GARDNER
130 Best-Selling Home Plans

FEATURES

HOME PLANS

HOW TO ORDER

Then and Now

Donald A. Gardner Architects, Inc., creates homes with classic appeal and an eye towards the desires of today's families.

by Paula Powers

WHEN DONALD A. GARDNER, AIA, NCARB STARTED DESIGNING PRE-designed house plans in 1978, his main goal was to elevate the quality of life for his homeowners. Now, over 20 years later, his impact on the house plan industry and housing trends across the nation is being realized. Don wasn't the first person to design portfolio house plans, but by extensive research into the way people really lived, along with the determination that affordable housing could be both functional and beautiful, he established a higher design standard based on tried-and-true architectural principles and his own ideas.

LEFT: Donald A. Gardner Architects, Inc., is a family-owned business. Pictured are father and daughter, CEO Donald A. Gardner, AIA, NCARB and President Angela Santerini. ABOVE: Showcasing old country style, this beautiful farmhouse— HPT910010—offers a modern, family-efficient floor plan. See page 50 for details.

Like all great stories, there were many obstacles to overcome in order for Donald A. Gardner Architects, Inc., to be where it is today. The first was a discouraging professor who warned Don that residential design wouldn't be a rewarding career, but perhaps the biggest challenges were other designers who said that what Don wanted to do couldn't be done. Still, Don knew where his talents and interests were. After graduating from Clemson University with a degree in architecture, serving two years in the Army Corp of Engineers, and working for large and small architectural firms designing industrial, institutional, commercial, and residential projects, Don founded Donald A. Gardner Architects, Inc., as a part-time home-based business.

While designing home plans in his spare time, Don decided to use well-placed magazine ads to publicize his designs. Believing the needs and wishes of homebuyers—not the housing industry—should dictate affordable housing, along with refusing to sacrifice curb appeal or custom features, his ideas, research, and determination were worth his effort. Homebuyers embraced his designs, and gradually Don devoted more

TOP: Believing rear exteriors should also be striking, Donald A. Gardner Architects, Inc., incorporates features such as: dormers, columns, and French doors. ABOVE: Combining gentle curves and sharp lines for stunning curb appeal, the brick facade surrounds an open floor plan with custom-styled features. (Plan HPT910003; see page 44 for details.)

of his attention to Donald A. Gardner Architects, Inc., turning it into more than a part-time venture. "We offered volume spaces inside and a nicely detailed, balanced, attractive exterior in a production plan," said Don, "and it just took off."

With the help of his wife, children, and a small startup staff, Donald A. Gardner Architects, Inc., has grown into a national full-service architecture firm and created additional sister companies such as:

Donald A. Gardner Interactive; Allora, LLC; and Infringement Solutions. Today, with the assistance of his grown children, Angela Santerini and Donald Gardner Jr., and son-in-law, Bill Santerini, as well as nearly fifty full-time employees, Donald A. Gardner Architects, Inc., has become a well-known and respected residential architecture firm, and Don has earned the reputation of being a leading residential architect of pre-designed house plans.

ABOUT THE DESIGNER

In 1994, Donald A. Gardner Builders was established, and in 2002, it merged with a number of registered architects and industry specialists to form Allora, LLC. Allora, LLC is a land planning, design and construction firm that focuses on high-end custom projects, including single and multi-family residences, amenity facilities, and light commercial assignments. From an individual house to an entire development, Allora works as a single unit from concept to completion, making each aspect of the process easier for their client. "When we can help with every aspect of the building experi-

TOP: Allora, LLC meets developer needs with multi-family residences that offer open floor plans and custom features, while blending with their environment. ABOVE LEFT: Allora, LLC offers land planning, which showcases natural features and views. ABOVE RIGHT: Offering high-end custom design, Allora, LLC incorporates the requirements and wishes of homeowners with careful consideration to the surrounding community and environment.

ence from start to finish, from the first glimmer of an idea to the finished product," said Don, "then we know we have done our job."

Also in 2002, Infringement Solutions was established. An award-winning architect is often imitated, but occasionally, his or her work is copied. In order to

reduce and deter the number of copyright violations against architects and designers, Infringement Solutions pursues cases involving offenders. With Donald A. Gardner Architects, Inc., and a number of top designers as their clients, Infringement Solutions is paving the way for copyright education and protection in the home plan industry.

It isn't hard to see why Donald A. Gardner Architects Inc., is an industry favorite. "Everything we do centers around our clients. We have diversified in order to fulfill all of our clients' needs and desires," said President Angela Santerini. "We didn't want them to have to run here and there when it's easier to get the products and services they need all in one place."

This devotion to their clients has earned them over forty awards and honors in a broad range of categories. Their clients have shown appreciation for the attention Donald A. Gardner Architects, Inc., has given to the way people live and what their requirements and wishes are. In fact, over 100,000 Don Gardner homes have been built nationwide and in 18 vastly different countries.

Some say it's the open, family-efficient floor plans; some say it's the beautiful, low-maintenance exteriors. Others would argue that it's the custom features that were once reserved for the rich, and others would argue that it's the affordability. For these reasons and more, Donald A. Gardner Architects, Inc., is a consumer favorite. "I'm happy people choose to live in our homes," said Don. "We want to raise the quality of life for our homeowners; that includes accommodating active lifestyles and providing flexible spaces for a family's changing needs."

"Being a family-owned business, families and how they live are very important to us," said Angela. "We're big believers in research, and we are constantly looking for ways to improve living." This commitment is echoed by the employees, so homebuyers can look forward to a home that will adapt to them and for more great things to come from Donald A. Gardner Architects, Inc., in the future. ■

ABOVE TOP: CEO of Donald A. Gardner Architects, Inc., Donald A. Gardner, AIA, NCARB.
ABOVE: President of Donald A. Gardner Architects, Inc., Angela Santerini.

Attractive and affordable, this one-level home offers a bonus room for expansion purposes and porches conducive to outdoor entertaining. Plan HPT910012; see page 54 for details.

timeless quality

Combining the classic design features of
days gone by with today's hottest amenities,
this traditional home offers the best of both worlds.

THIS STATELY BRICK FACADE FEATURES A COLUMNED, COVERED FRONT PORCH
that ushers visitors into the large foyer. The dormer window above the
entry echoes two dormers that accent the garage. Two Palladian windows
not only add character to the front of the home but also bathe the interior
in natural light. An expansive great room with a fireplace, a cathedral
ceiling, and access to a covered rear porch sits in a central location and acts
as a convenient hub for the entire plan.

*ABOVE: Contributing brightness and the feeling of spaciousness, the Palladian
window in the study acts as a fine backdrop for a desk. LEFT: While numerous
dormers and gables accent this home, Palladian windows provide additional
distinction to the exterior's facade.*

Though loaded with open, casual space, the plan also allows for formal entertaining when the occasion arises. The dining room features a unique ceiling treatment and decorative defining columns; it is capacious enough for elegant formal parties and is ideally situated right next to the kitchen.

Plenty of counter and cabinet space makes cooking and entertaining at home easy. A gourmet's dream, the open kitchen is also within easy reach of the great room and breakfast area. A wall of windows adorns the breakfast area, overlooking the deck out back. To the left of the breakfast area, a door to the rear porch provides easy access to the spacious deck, ideal for barbecues on warm summer nights. The porch, also accessible via the great room, has skylights—thus making it a cozy space, even during the winter months.

No cook could resist the workspace in the kitchen. White cabinets and sand countertops lend a sense of cleanliness and order.

Hardwood floors unite the great room and breakfast nook. French doors flanked by long windows look out on the backyard.

Grand in design and area, the dining room is large enough to hold a sideboard as well as a table and chairs. Elegant ceiling detail complements a stylish chandelier.

Skylights also brighten the many appointments in the master bath: a corner spa tub, dual sinks, and a separate shower. Split-bedroom planning places the fine master bath and master bedroom to the right of the home, providing privacy for the homeowners. The master suite also includes a walk-in closet.

Two bedrooms with abundant closet space reside to the left of the plan. An optional bedroom or study with a tray ceiling and Palladian window faces the front of the home. A half-bath near the study makes it a convenient optional suite for overnight guests.

The utility room provides space for a washer and dryer, plus built-in cabinets, and is located right next to the two-car garage. Access the garage via a service entry, situated between the dining room and master suite. The two-story garage contains extra room for storage and provides bonus space on the second floor, which could easily be transformed into a game room or exercise room at a future time. ■

plan# HPT910008

- STYLE: TRADITIONAL
- SQUARE FOOTAGE: 2,625
- BONUS SPACE: 447 SQ. FT.
- BEDROOMS: 4
- BATHROOMS: 2½
- WIDTH: 63'-1"
- DEPTH: 90'-2"

SEARCH ONLINE @ EPLANS.COM

natural blend

Different exterior styles combine perfectly in this lovely one-level home, which will fit well in any neighborhood.

LOOKING FOR SUBTLY SENSATIONAL? THIS WELL-PLANNED design hits the mark perfectly, inside and out. Featuring a stunning exterior of stucco, stone, and cedar shakes, this home blends with and takes advantage of the beauty of its natural surroundings. Plenty of windows and an expansive covered porch to the rear of the plan add even more benefits, allowing family and guests to move easily between indoors and outdoors.

Above: Columns and dormer windows lend country charm to the rear porch. Opposite: This enchanting home boasts curb appeal with its stone and stucco facade.

The luxurious great room has an enlarged fireplace and high ceilings.

The rear of the house has extended windows, allowing natural light to brighten every room.

Designed for optimum openness, the living spaces of the plan boast elegant touches such as columns, which define the foyer, and soaring ceiling heights—a cathedral ceiling enhances the great room, and the foyer and dining room feature 10-foot ceilings. The great room also includes a fireplace, built-in bookshelves, and a curved wall of windows that overlooks the covered rear porch. The kitchen, with a U-shaped countertop, shares a snack bar with the great room and opens to the porch. The nearby breakfast nook, with three full walls of windows, serves as a bright spot for casual family meals.

Sleeping quarters here are just as captivating as the living spaces. The stately master suite, with a tray ceiling, contains two walk-in closets and a private bath with two vanities, a linen closet, a compartmented toilet, and a spa tub set under a window. This suite also boasts a private sitting area, as well as access to the porch. Two additional bedrooms complete the plan; one, with a private bath, sits to the left of the plan, and the other, located at the front of the plan, doubles as a study. ■

The master suite includes dual vanities and a relaxing soaking tub overlooking the yard.

PORCH

BRKFST.
9-8 x 9-8

SITTING
9-8 x 6-4

(cathedral ceiling)

BED RM.
13-0 x 14-4

KITCHEN
12-6 x 11-0

GREAT RM.
20-0 x 18-0

MASTER
BED RM.
16-0 x 14-4

fireplace

walk-in closet

bath

UTIL.
8-8 x 6-0

walk-in closet

lin.

FOYER
6-11 x 9-5
(10' ceiling)

bath

master bath

DINING
12-0 x 13-8
(10' ceiling)

BED RM./
STUDY
12-4 x 13-0

GARAGE
21-4 x 22-6

PORCH

© 1998 DONALD A. GARDNER
All rights reserved

plan# HPT910002

- STYLE: TRADITIONAL
- SQUARE FOOTAGE: 2,201
- BEDROOMS: 3
- BATHROOMS: 3
- WIDTH: 69'-6"
- DEPTH: 55'-10"

SEARCH ONLINE @ EPLANS.COM

The covered porch and centered gable above provide a welcoming facade on this gorgeous three-bedroom home.

bright ideas

Natural light is as much a fixture in this house as the walls themselves. A multitude of windows illuminates the spacious interior, revealing the special details found within.

A CHARMING EXTERIOR, COMPOSED OF SIDING WITH STONE ACCENTS, IS ONLY THE BEGINNING OF this captivating multi-level design. Though the stone adds a rustic touch to the facade, arched windows topped by keystone lintels add a touch of elegance, and the wide front porch provides a country welcome.

ABOVE: Marble countertops and a built-in wine rack create an elegant aura in the kitchen. OPPOSITE PAGE: A Palladian window and a soaring cathedral ceiling enhance the great room, which boasts a hardwood floor.

Inside, the foyer includes a coat closet and easily accesses a nearby powder room—a convenient layout for families that enjoy entertaining guests. The central great room serves as an excellent gathering spot; a fireplace makes the room even more welcoming, and a cathedral ceiling adds grandeur. The covered rear porch is accessible from the great

room as well as the adjacent dining room, which is located to the rear of the plan and features a bay window designed to take advantage of sweeping views. The kitchen and breakfast area create a charming informal space. The kitchen's open floor plan allows easy service to both the dining room and breakfast area, and a walk-in pantry just around the

corner provides extra storage space. The breakfast room, brightened by a tall triple window, opens to a small side porch.

The right side of the plan is devoted to the resplendent master suite. A bay window brings natural light into the master bedroom, which boasts a tray ceiling. The lavish master bath, also with a tray ceiling, includes a double vanity,

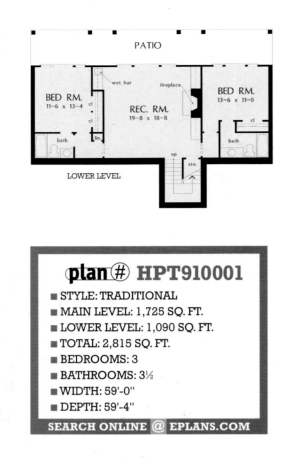

LOWER LEVEL

MAIN LEVEL

©1999 Donald A. Gardner, Inc.

plan# HPT910001

- **STYLE:** TRADITIONAL
- **MAIN LEVEL:** 1,725 SQ. FT.
- **LOWER LEVEL:** 1,090 SQ. FT.
- **TOTAL:** 2,815 SQ. FT.
- **BEDROOMS:** 3
- **BATHROOMS:** 3½
- **WIDTH:** 59'-0"
- **DEPTH:** 59'-4"

SEARCH ONLINE @ EPLANS.COM

an oval soaking tub, a compartmented toilet, and a shower with a built-in seat. Two walk-in closets complete this suite.

Two additional bedrooms join a recreation room on the lower level; each bedroom includes a private bath, and both open to the patio. Special features in the recreation room, which also opens to the patio, include a wet bar, a fireplace, and built-in shelves. ■

The bay window in the master suite takes advantage of a striking outdoor view.

TO ORDER BLUEPRINTS CALL TOLL FREE 1-800-521-6797

A soaring double-door entry is the focal point of this distinguished traditional home.

room to grow

Enter this elegant four-bedroom home through the two-story foyer and marvel at the flawless interior—complete with 308 sq. ft. of bonus space!

TRADITIONAL STYLE TAKES A LOVELY MODERN TURN IN THIS CHARMING FOUR-BEDROOM HOME. THIS HOME SHOWCASES PLENTY of windows, allowing the rooms to take advantage of natural light—dormer, bay, and box-bay are only a few of the window styles displayed throughout the home. Originally designed with a stucco exterior to add European charm, these homeowners chose a brick facade, giving the home a more classic look. The timeless exterior gives way to an interior that highlights some of today's favorite amenities, including a flowing floor plan with fireplaces, easy outdoor access, and even some home office/flex space.

The first floor begins with the two-story foyer—entered through elegant double doors—which offers a nearby coat closet. To the left of the foyer, the living room/study boasts a box-bay window and a fireplace, and the dining room to the right includes a wall of windows. Highlights in the spacious family room include a second fireplace, built-in shelves, and access to the rear patio. The open floor plan allows views of the kitchen and breakfast nook too. A bay window provides natural light in the breakfast nook, while the kitchen contains a center work island with a double sink and a snack bar.

A petite pantry, just outside the kitchen, allows convenient service to the dining room. Just beyond the kitchen, a versatile room with an adjacent private bath can serve as a home office or an extra bedroom. The laundry area is discretely placed near the garage, next to a powder room. The master suite resides in the opposite wing; luxurious features here include a bayed sitting area, a large walk-in closet, and a private bath with dual sinks, an oval tub, and a compartmented toilet.

Upstairs, two bedrooms and a bonus room share a balcony that overlooks the family room. The bedrooms share a linen closet and a private bath with dual sinks, and both include a walk-in closet. The slightly sunken bonus room, big enough for a game or recreation room, boasts a dormer alcove. ∎

White cabinetry in the kitchen contrasts nicely with the striking black countertop and dark wallpaper.

FEATURE DESIGNS

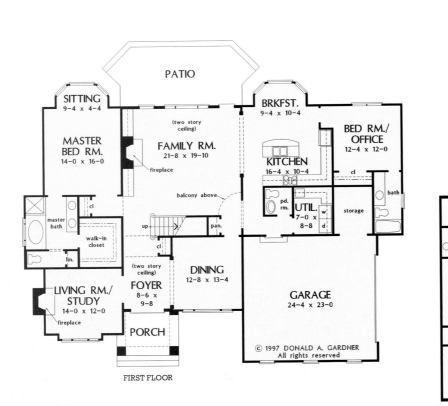

PATIO

SITTING
9-4 x 4-4

MASTER
BED RM.
14-0 x 16-0

FAMILY RM.
21-8 x 19-10

(two story ceiling)

fireplace

balcony above

master bath

cl

walk-in closet

lin.

BRKFST.
9-4 x 10-4

KITCHEN
16-4 x 10-4

BED RM./OFFICE
12-4 x 12-0

cl

bath

pd. rm.

UTIL.
7-0 x 8-8

w
d

storage

up

(two story ceiling)

cl

pan.

DINING
12-8 x 13-4

GARAGE
24-4 x 23-0

LIVING RM./STUDY
14-0 x 12-0

fireplace

FOYER
8-6 x 9-8

PORCH

© 1997 DONALD A. GARDNER
All rights reserved

FIRST FLOOR

plan # HPT910005

- STYLE: TRADITIONAL
- FIRST FLOOR: 2,249 SQ. FT.
- SECOND FLOOR: 620 SQ. FT.
- TOTAL: 2,869 SQ. FT.
- BONUS SPACE: 308 SQ. FT.
- BEDROOMS: 4
- BATHROOMS: 3½
- WIDTH: 69'-6"
- DEPTH: 52'-0"

SEARCH ONLINE @ EPLANS.COM

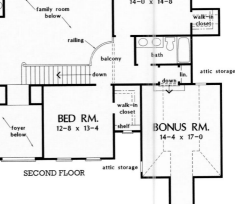

family room below

railing

balcony

down

BED RM.
14-0 x 14-8

walk-in closet

bath

lin.

attic storage

foyer below

BED RM.
12-8 x 13-4

walk-in closet

shelf

down

BONUS RM.
14-4 x 17-0

attic storage

SECOND FLOOR

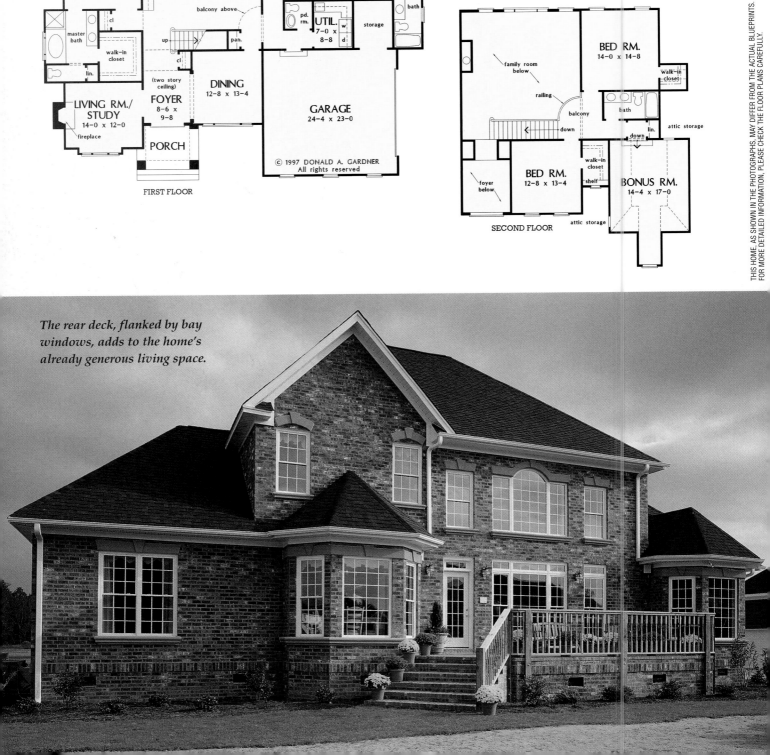

The rear deck, flanked by bay windows, adds to the home's already generous living space.

A hardwood floor and a splendid selection of plants highlight the great room's connection with nature.

small wonder

This enchanting three-bedroom house boasts an amenity-packed design that is usually reserved for much larger homes.

THIS HOME'S ABUNDANT CURB APPEAL SETS THE TONE FOR THE REST OF THE PLAN. COZY, YET boasting all the elegant luxuries that distinguish this home from the rest, it includes a spacious front porch, two-car garage, and even a cathedral ceiling. A vast array of windows illuminate the interior, maximizing the floor plan by providing sweeping views of the outdoor property. The country feel combines with a modern layout usually found in much larger homes. Family and friends are greeted by a covered front porch that gives way to a foyer flanked by an elegant dining room and a versatile room that can be used as a bedroom or study.

The dining room is conveniently close to the kitchen, so meals can be easily whisked in and out while guests await the next course. The gourmet kitchen provides lots of storage and counter space for the family chef to utilize. Casual meals can be enjoyed in the breakfast room, which features views of the backyard, courtesy of a ribbon of windows that separate the room from the convenient rear porch.

The proximity of the rear porch to the breakfast room and kitchen welcomes outdoor meals.

The lavish master suite, complete with a walk-in closet and direct access to the rear deck, is nestled in the rear of the right wing of the plan, as homeowners relish their privacy from the rest of the bedrooms. A tray ceiling makes the spacious room appear even larger, adding a unique touch to the romantic atmosphere. The master bath boasts a skylight, illuminating the luxurious whirlpool tub. The utility area is conveniently located just outside the master bedroom.

The stunning great room — enhanced by a cathedral ceiling in addition to a clerestory window — bathes the room in light. The large great

LEFT: A welcoming front porch is indicative of the timeless style that makes this three-bedroom home irresistible. ABOVE: The dining room is flanked by columns and enjoys sunlight and views of the front yard.

room is graced with a fireplace, which brings a cozy feel, evident when entertaining a crowd or while spending a quiet evening at home. The spacious room also enjoys direct access to the rear porch.

Beyond the great room is a family bedroom, complete with a walk-in closet and adjacent bath. The room also enjoys views of the backyard via the rear porch.

When entering into the home via the two-car garage, one goes through the utility room, which can almost be used as a mudroom to avoid sloshing through the foyer on a rainy day.

Two spacious outdoor porches, a two-car garage, a lavish master bath, and even an elegant great room with a cathedral ceiling—all wrapped up neatly into a single floor! Leave the hassle of constant stair traffic behind, without compromising versatility and luxury. This always-in-style classic is sure to please even the most discriminating of tastes and leave owners wondering how they could have ever settled for living in anything less. ∎

Showing why it is indeed called the great room, this space boasts a fireplace and a cathedral ceiling, in addition to access to the rear porch.

plan# HPT910009

- **STYLE:** COUNTRY
- **SQUARE FOOTAGE:** 1,632
- **BEDROOMS:** 3
- **BATHS:** 2
- **WIDTH:** 62'-4"
- **DEPTH:** 55'-2"

SEARCH ONLINE @ EPLANS.COM

The rear porch is the perfect place for get-togethers while enjoying the outdoors.

PORCH

BED RM.
11-4 x 11-0

(cathedral ceiling)
GREAT RM.
15-4 x 18-6

fireplace

bath

walk-in closet

BED RM./
STUDY
11-0 x 11-8

FOYER
6-0 x 8-4

DINING
11-0 x 11-8

storage

BRKFST.
10-4 x 8-8

KIT.
11-4 x 12-10

MASTER
BED RM.
13-4 x 16-4

master bath

skylight

walk-in closet

storage

UTIL.

GARAGE
21-0 x 21-8

© 1995 DONALD A. GARDNER
All rights reserved
(optional door location)

PORCH

QUOTE ONE®
Cost to build? See page 186
to order complete cost estimate
to build this house in your area!

simple pleasure

Gables, arched windows, and a stone-and-wood exterior work together to give this home an appealing character.

This stunning three-bedroom home offers aesthetically pleasing touches and a functional design.

FOUR GABLES PROVIDE A ROOFLINE AS DISTINCTIVE AS AN ALPS MOUNTAIN RANGE, HIGHLIGHTING the exterior of this unique, European-inspired design. Arched windows, quaint shutters, and inviting steps to the front porch work together to give this home an impressive facade—a specific goal of the design, according to architect Donald A. Gardner.

The great room, complete with a commanding fireplace, can be viewed from the upstairs hall.

The free-flowing design of this spacious dining room is perfect for entertaining.

"This home fits in a compact package, but was designed to look and live much bigger," Gardner said. "Multiple gables in front, as tall as two stories, give the house a larger feel, and the entry, balanced at the center of the house, has added height and importance."

Guests enter the three-bedroom, two-and-a-half bath home through the two-story foyer, which looks into the formal dining room on the right. A small hallway ahead draws visitors into the great room, the center of attention in the home.

The spacious great room is sure to be a hub of activity, whether relaxing with family or hosting a party. Its open design is connected to nearly every corner of the house, from the second-floor balcony overlook to the French doors leading to the backyard patio.

"The great room ceiling features intersecting vaults, which make the space more dramatic," Gardner said. "The expansive, arched transom on the vaulted rear wall accentuates the volume and makes the room feel larger.

The breakfast nook is conveniently located between the great room and kitchen.

The master suite features a walk-in closet, and a comforting bath.

This, combined with the second-floor overlook and open breakfast room, results in only one solid wall and a room that stretches into adjacent spaces and to the outdoors."

A large fireplace warms the great room in the winter, and built-in cabinets to either side add style and convenience. Natural light pours in through the French doors and windows on the back wall. Another door and even more windows grace the breakfast nook, which conveniently links the great room and kitchen.

Every meal will be easy to prepare in the kitchen, thanks to its generous counter space, intelligent design, and perfect location. Nestled between the dining room and breakfast nook, the kitchen can conveniently serve both of those rooms—or meals on the patio or at the snack bar.

The entire right side of the plan is devoted to the master suite, with privacy that belies its convenient location immediately off the great room. A tray ceiling in the bedroom is consistent with the home's airy feel, and the walk-in closet and bath promise to pamper the homeowner.

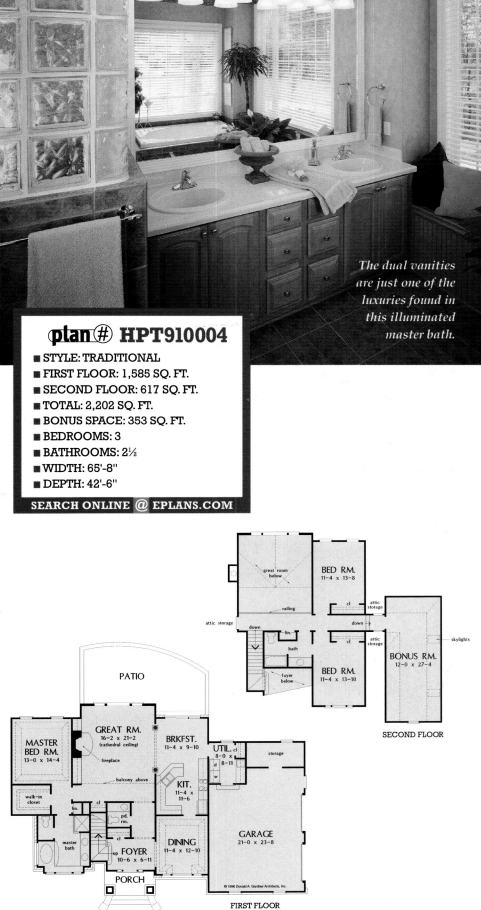

The dual vanities are just one of the luxuries found in this illuminated master bath.

plan# HPT910004

- STYLE: TRADITIONAL
- FIRST FLOOR: 1,585 SQ. FT.
- SECOND FLOOR: 617 SQ. FT.
- TOTAL: 2,202 SQ. FT.
- BONUS SPACE: 353 SQ. FT.
- BEDROOMS: 3
- BATHROOMS: 2½
- WIDTH: 65'-8"
- DEPTH: 42'-6"

SEARCH ONLINE @ EPLANS.COM

THIS HOME, AS SHOWN IN THE PHOTOGRAPHS, MAY DIFFER FROM THE ACTUAL BLUEPRINTS. FOR MORE DETAILED INFORMATION, PLEASE CHECK THE FLOOR PLANS CAREFULLY.

Upstairs offers the great room over-look, leading to a pair of bedrooms that share a full bath. A large bonus room, accented by two skylights, provides room to grow, while the plan also offers ample attic storage space.

That additional space adds to the comfort level that exists throughout the home—from the vaulted ceilings in the great room to the relaxing master suite. ■

country time

With a wraparound front porch and three dormers above, this home promises relaxing country living.

FEW HOMES EMBRACE THE BEAUTY OF AN OPEN LANDSCAPE AS WELL AS THE CLASSIC design featured in this delightful retreat. The welcoming charm of this country farmhouse is expressed by its many windows and its covered wraparound porch. A two-story entrance foyer is enhanced by a Palladian window in a clerestory dormer above to let in natural lighting. The first-floor master suite allows privacy and accessibility. The lavish master bath includes a whirlpool tub, separate shower, a double-bowl vanity, and a walk-in closet. The first floor features nine-foot ceilings throughout with the exception of the kitchen area, which sports an eight-foot ceiling. The second floor contains two additional bedrooms, a full bath and plenty of storage space. The bonus room provides room to grow.

ABOVE: Hardwood floors and an open floor plan contribute to the appeal inside this beautiful farmhouse. The modern layout enables family and friends to move throughout the home with ease, as the rooms effortlessly flow into one another. LEFT: Let your cares gently glide away on this front porch, with ample space for rocking chairs, a porch swing, or even both.

Beyond the welcoming wraparound porch, the spacious foyer is the tour guide of the house. From there, family and friends will congregate in the great room, complete with a grand fireplace, or head straight back to the kitchen and breakfast area for some country fare.

The kitchen's white cabinets and beige countertops are brightened by the natural light shining through from the rear deck. The accessibility of the spacious outdoor deck from the kitchen and breakfast room provides an enticing invitation for outside dining on warm mornings or tranquil evenings. On the other side of the kitchen is the dining area, enabling the chef to easily retrieve last-minute trimmings for dinner. The room follows the same color scheme as the kitchen and breakfast room: beige walls with white moulding. The dining area is the perfect size to entertain guests or have an intimate dinner with the family.

The elegant dining area opens to the great room via a spacious entrance way. Wood floors in rich tones complement the crisp white color of the fireplace and bookshelves. Oversized couches and deep accents, such as end tables or a leather chair, serve as the last ingredients for a relaxing read in front of the fire.

Opposite the great room is the master bedroom, which provides more than enough space for the owners of the house. The bedroom leads to a huge walk-in closet which is big enough for both to share. The luxurious master suite also contains a wondrous master bath equipped with a whirlpool tub, a separate shower, and even a double bowl vanity. The first floor is completed with a side-entrance garage.

Two more bedrooms boast double closets, and are located on the second floor of the house. A full bath is conveniently stationed between the rooms, providing efficiency for the children of the house or overnight guests. There is also ample attic storage space in addition to a bonus room that can be converted into a bedroom or media room. ∎

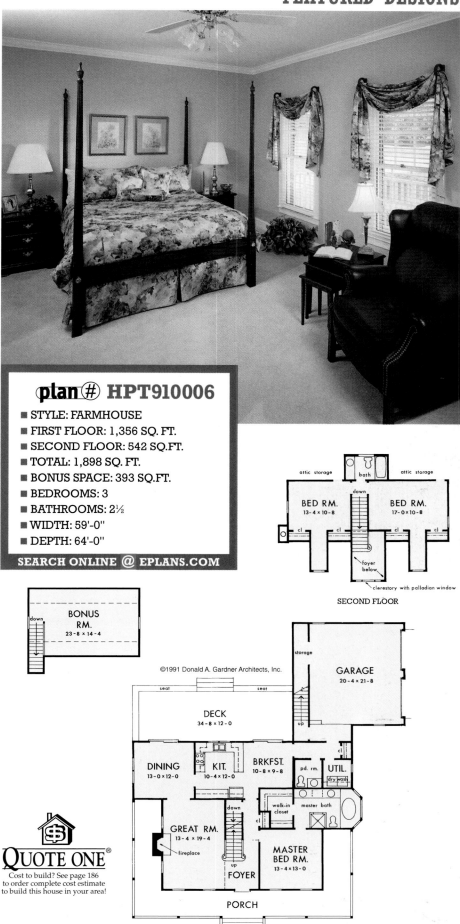

plan # HPT910006

- **STYLE:** FARMHOUSE
- **FIRST FLOOR:** 1,356 SQ. FT.
- **SECOND FLOOR:** 542 SQ. FT.
- **TOTAL:** 1,898 SQ. FT.
- **BONUS SPACE:** 393 SQ. FT.
- **BEDROOMS:** 3
- **BATHROOMS:** 2½
- **WIDTH:** 59'-0"
- **DEPTH:** 64'-0"

SEARCH ONLINE @ EPLANS.COM

SECOND FLOOR

BONUS RM.
23-8 × 14-4

©1991 Donald A. Gardner Architects, Inc.

QUOTE ONE®
Cost to build? See page 186 to order complete cost estimate to build this house in your area!

FIRST FLOOR

twin peaks

Symmetrical gables flank the entrance to this traditional four-bedroom home.

CLASSIC SYMMETRY CHARACTERIZES THIS HOME, WHICH FEATURES LARGE ARCHED windows, round columns, a covered porch, and brick veneer siding. Corner quoins and shutters broaden the traditional influence. The arched window in the clerestory above the entrance provides natural light to the interior. A family-sized floor plan offers flexible livability and comfort without being ostentatious. The great room boasts a cathedral ceiling, a fireplace, and built-in cabinets and bookshelves. Intended as a central gathering space for both formal and informal occasions, the great room is spacious enough to handle quiet family evenings as well as glamorous parties.

LEFT: Between the corner quoins, the large arched windows, and round columns, the attention to detail in this design is what makes the end result so spectacular. ABOVE: The sunroom and deck lie beyond the great room, providing a graceful transition to the promise of outdoor living.

ABOVE: The arched clerestory window and cathedral ceiling make the sunroom one of the highlights of this beautiful home. RIGHT: Use the front room, with its Palladian window and tray ceiling, as a study, den, or extra bedroom.

Doors lead to the sunroom, which has an arched transom over the French doors leading out to the deck. Build the deck as shown with a spa for easy relaxation. The L-shaped kitchen serves the dining room, the breakfast area, and the great room and also boasts an island counter for quick meals.

The master suite, with a fireplace, maintains a private passage to the deck and its spa. Its attendant bath has all the items you're looking for: a spa tub, a

separate shower, dual sinks, and a linen closet. Three additional bedrooms—one could serve as a study—are at the other end of the house for privacy. One even has a walk-in closet.

The spacious two-car garage contains two separate storage areas and provides convenient access to the kitchen. Bonus space over the garage can be developed later into an office, hobby space, or anything the homeowner desires. ■

ABOVE: Columns provide an elegant division between the great room and kitchen. LEFT: Elevate the back deck and this plan can work perfectly on a sloped lot. RIGHT: The master bedroom provides a private entrance to the back deck; it also boasts a walk-in closet.

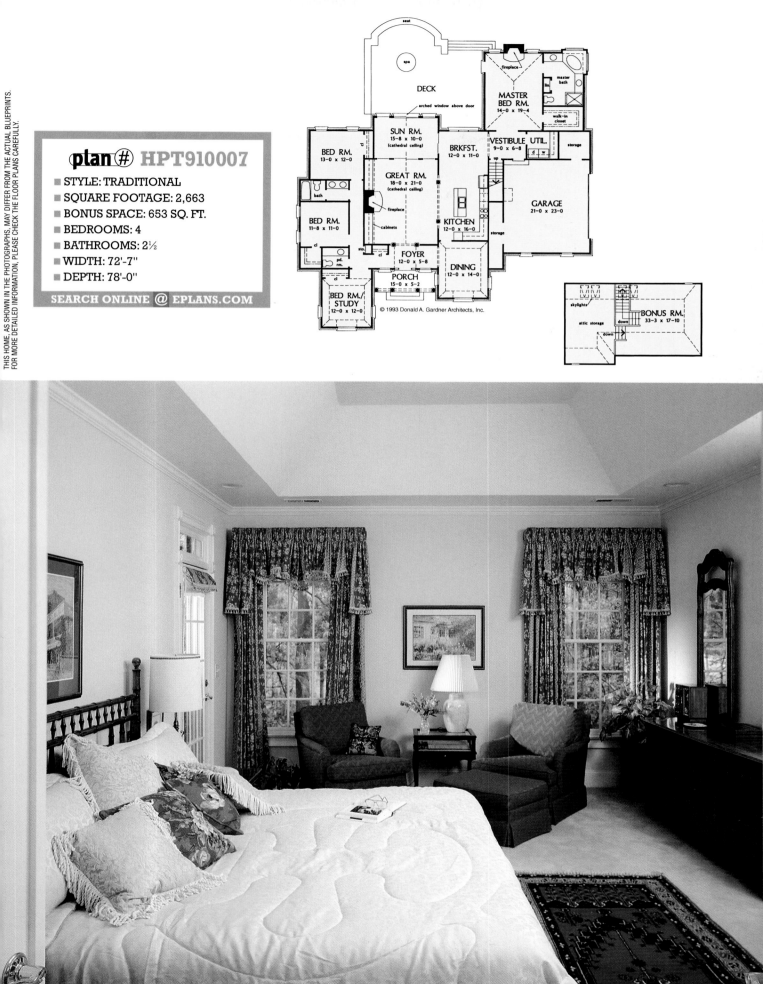

plan# HPT910007

- **STYLE:** TRADITIONAL
- **SQUARE FOOTAGE:** 2,663
- **BONUS SPACE:** 653 SQ. FT.
- **BEDROOMS:** 4
- **BATHROOMS:** 2½
- **WIDTH:** 72'-7"
- **DEPTH:** 78'-0"

SEARCH ONLINE @ EPLANS.COM

DECK

seat

spa

SUN RM.
15-8 x 10-0
(cathedral ceiling)

arched window above door

BED RM.
13-0 x 12-0

cl

bath

BED RM.
11-8 x 11-0

GREAT RM.
18-0 x 21-0
(cathedral ceiling)

fireplace

cabinets

sto.

cl

cl

pd.
rm.

cl

FOYER
12-0 x 5-8

PORCH
15-0 x 5-2

BED RM./
STUDY
12-0 x 12-0

BRKFST.
12-0 x 11-0

KITCHEN
12-0 x 16-0

DINING
12-0 x 14-0

fireplace

MASTER
BED RM.
14-0 x 19-4

master
bath

lin.

walk-in
closet

VESTIBULE UTIL.
9-0 x 6-8

d w

storage

up

storage

GARAGE
21-0 x 23-0

© 1993 Donald A. Gardner Architects, Inc.

skylights

attic storage

down

down

BONUS RM.
33-3 x 17-10

subtle luxury

Impressive but not ostentatious, there's a lot to love about this three-bedroom traditional home. It's unique layout is both sumptuous and fuctional.

KEYSTONE ARCHES, INK-BLACK SHUTTERS, AND A CHARMING EYEBROW DORMER ADD elegance to this symmetrical design. A carved front door, flanked by etched-glass sidelights, provides an eye-catching centerpiece to its distinguished brick facade, while flower boxes, just below the second-floor windows, add a touch of country whimsy.

LEFT: A central island with a sink provides a convenient workspace in the spacious kitchen. ABOVE: Arch-topped windows on the first floor with even larger windows above hint at the natural light that bathes the interior.

Living spaces inside offer a distinctive blend of formal and informal, and an open floor plan allows views from one room to the next. A cozy study, perfect for a home office, and a chic dining room border the foyer, which includes a coat closet and is naturally lit by a double clerestory window.

A fireplace, built-in bookshelves, and two sets of French doors that open to the rear porch make the vaulted two-story great room a wonderful gathering area—a snack bar, shared with the roomy island kitchen, allows this room to serve as a place for casual meals as well. The breakfast room, adjacent to the kitchen, extends into a bright bay; just around the corner are a built-in planning

Vivid reds, dark woods and a central fireplace add warmth to the great room; note the views of the kitchen and dining room.

Brilliant colors, sheer curtains and a crystal chandelier create a hospitable atmosphere in the dining room.

A tall arched window brings natural light to the study, which has been transformed into a distinguished home office.

desk and walk-in pantry. Extra storage space is available in the garage, and the utility area is discreetly tucked away behind the dining room.

Comfortable luxury defines the sleeping quarters here; the first-floor

Hardwood floors, a fireplace and tall windows make the master bedroom a grand retreat.

plan# HPT910003

- STYLE: TRADITIONAL
- FIRST FLOOR: 2,270 SQ. FT.
- SECOND FLOOR: 685 SQ. FT.
- TOTAL: 2,955 SQ. FT.
- BONUS SPACE: 563 SQ. FT.
- BEDROOMS: 3
- BATHROOMS: 2½
- WIDTH: 75'-1"
- DEPTH: 53'-6"

SEARCH ONLINE @ EPLANS.COM

SECOND FLOOR

- BONUS RM. 15-0 x 28-4
- storage
- attic storage
- great room below
- railing
- walk-in closet
- down
- down
- bath
- attic storage
- walk-in closet
- attic storage
- BED RM. 13-0 x 12-0
- foyer below
- BED RM. 13-0 x 12-0

FIRST FLOOR

- PATIO
- STORAGE 10-4 x 6-4
- desk
- pantry
- BRKFST. 13-4 x 12-0
- PORCH
- fireplace
- MASTER BED RM. 16-0 x 17-0
- fireplace
- ovens
- KITCHEN 13-4 x 12-8
- GREAT RM. 20-0 x 16-0 (vaulted ceiling)
- shelves
- walk-in closet
- walk-in closet
- GARAGE 22-0 x 31-0
- balcony above
- pd. rm.
- lin.
- master bath
- UTIL. 6-0 x 10-0
- © 2000 DAG All rights reserved
- sto.
- up
- DINING 13-0 x 12-0
- FOYER 8-0 x 12-8
- STUDY 13-0 x 12-0
- PORCH

master suite, highlighted by a tray ceiling, includes a fireplace, two walk-in closets, and a private bath with two vanities, a whirlpool tub, and separate shower. Upstairs, two family bedrooms—both with walk-in closets—share a full dual-vanity bath and a balcony that overlooks the great room. A large bonus room, enhanced by three dormer windows, allows the home to grow with the family. ■

Plan HPT910011; see page 52 for details.

COUNTRY/FARMHOUSE
DESIGNS

Discover the open spaces, inviting porches, and classic elements in these plans that capture the spirit of the countryside.

This beautiful farmhouse, with its prominent twin gables and bays, adds just the right amount of country style. The master suite is quietly tucked away downstairs with no rooms directly above. The family cook will love the spacious U-shaped kitchen and adjoining bayed breakfast nook. A bonus room is easily accessible from the back stairs or from the second floor, where three large bedrooms share two full baths. Storage space abounds with walk-ins, half-shelves and linen closets. A curved balcony borders a versatile loft/study, which overlooks the stunning two-story family room.

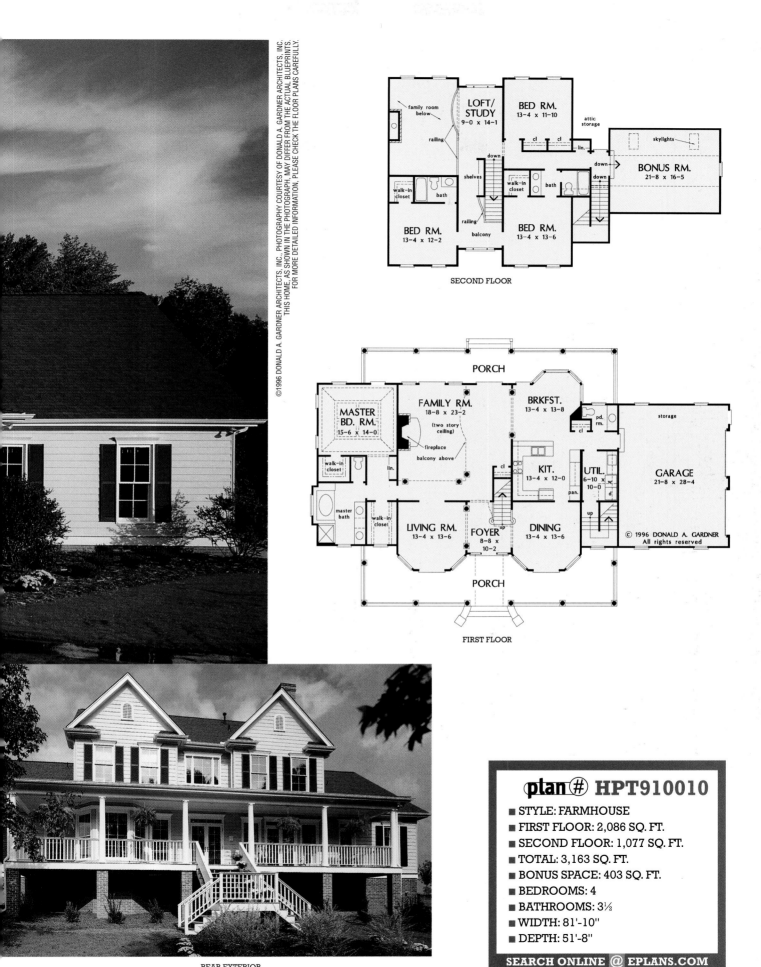

SECOND FLOOR

LOFT/STUDY 9-0 x 14-1
family room below
railing
BED RM. 13-4 x 11-10
attic storage
cl
lin.
skylights
BONUS RM. 21-8 x 16-5
down
down
down
walk-in closet
bath
shelves
walk-in closet
bath
BED RM. 13-4 x 12-2
railing
balcony
BED RM. 13-4 x 13-6

FIRST FLOOR

PORCH
MASTER BD. RM. 15-6 x 14-0
FAMILY RM. 18-8 x 23-2 (two story ceiling)
fireplace
balcony above
BRKFST. 13-4 x 13-8
pd. rm.
cl
storage
walk-in closet
lin.
cl
KIT. 13-4 x 12-0
pan.
UTIL. 6-10 x 10-0
w d
GARAGE 21-8 x 28-4
master bath
walk-in closet
LIVING RM. 13-4 x 13-6
FOYER 8-8 x 10-2
up
DINING 13-4 x 13-6
up
© 1996 Donald A. Gardner All rights reserved
PORCH

REAR EXTERIOR

plan# HPT910010

- STYLE: FARMHOUSE
- FIRST FLOOR: 2,086 SQ. FT.
- SECOND FLOOR: 1,077 SQ. FT.
- TOTAL: 3,163 SQ. FT.
- BONUS SPACE: 403 SQ. FT.
- BEDROOMS: 4
- BATHROOMS: 3½
- WIDTH: 81'-10"
- DEPTH: 51'-8"

SEARCH ONLINE @ EPLANS.COM

Three dormers top a very welcoming covered wraparound porch on this attractive country home. The entrance enjoys a Palladian clerestory window, lending an abundance of natural light to the foyer. The great room furthers this feeling of airiness with a balcony above and two sets of sliding glass doors leading to the back porch. For privacy, the master suite occupies the right side of the first floor. With a sitting bay and all the amenities of a modern master bath, this lavish retreat will be a welcome haven for the homeowner. Two family bedrooms reside upstairs, sharing a balcony overlook into the great room.

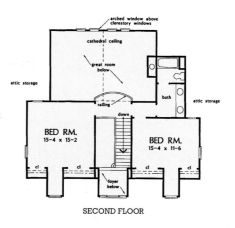

arched window above clerestory windows

cathedral ceiling

great room below

attic storage

railing

bath

attic storage

BED RM.
15-4 x 15-2

down

BED RM.
15-4 x 11-6

cl | cl

cl | cl

foyer below

SECOND FLOOR

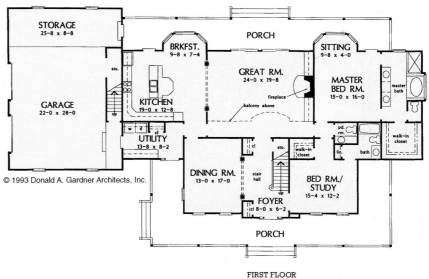

STORAGE
25-8 x 8-8

PORCH

BRKFST.
9-8 x 7-4

SITTING
9-8 x 4-0

sto.

GREAT RM.
24-0 x 19-8

GARAGE
22-0 x 28-0

KITCHEN
19-0 x 12-8

up

MASTER BED RM.
15-0 x 16-0

master bath

fireplace

balcony above

w | d

UTILITY
13-8 x 8-2

pd. rm.

walk-in closet

cl

sto.

walk-in closet

lin.

bath

DINING RM.
13-0 x 17-0

stair hall

up

BED RM./ STUDY
15-4 x 12-2

FOYER
cl 8-0 x 6-2

PORCH

© 1993 Donald A. Gardner Architects, Inc.

FIRST FLOOR

BONUS RM.
28-8 x 16-8

down

plan# HPT910011

- ■ STYLE: FARMHOUSE
- ■ FIRST FLOOR: 2,316 SQ. FT.
- ■ SECOND FLOOR: 721 SQ. FT.
- ■ TOTAL: 3,037 SQ. FT.
- ■ BONUS SPACE: 545 SQ. FT.
- ■ BEDROOMS: 4
- ■ BATHROOMS: 3½
- ■ WIDTH: 95'-4"
- ■ DEPTH: 54'-10"

SEARCH ONLINE @ EPLANS.COM

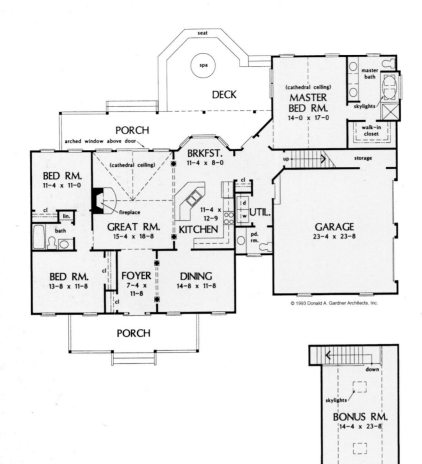

seat

spa

DECK

PORCH

arched window above door

(cathedral ceiling)

BED RM.
11-4 x 11-0

cl

lin.

bath

fireplace

GREAT RM.
15-4 x 18-8

BRKFST.
11-4 x 8-0

KITCHEN

11-4 x
12-9

cl

d
w

UTIL.

pd.
rm.

(cathedral ceiling)

MASTER
BED RM.
14-0 x 17-0

master
bath

skylights

walk-in
closet

up

storage

GARAGE
23-4 x 23-8

BED RM.
13-8 x 11-8

cl

FOYER
7-4 x
11-8

DINING
14-8 x 11-8

cl

PORCH

© 1993 Donald A. Gardner Architects, Inc.

down

skylights

BONUS RM.
14-4 x 23-8

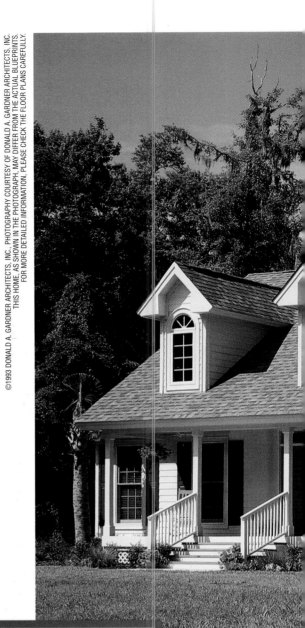

plan# HPT910012

- STYLE: FARMHOUSE
- SQUARE FOOTAGE: 1,864
- BONUS SPACE: 420 SQ. FT.
- BEDROOMS: 3
- BATHROOMS: 2½
- WIDTH: 71'-0"
- DEPTH: 56'-4"

SEARCH ONLINE @ EPLANS.COM

Quaint and cozy on the outside with porches front and back, this three-bedroom country home surprises with an open floor plan featuring a large great room with a cathedral ceiling. A central kitchen with an angled counter opens to the breakfast and great rooms for easy entertaining. The privately located master bedroom enjoys a cathedral ceiling and access to the deck. Two secondary bedrooms share a full hall bath. A bonus room makes expanding easy.

Dormers, arched windows and covered porches lend this home its country appeal. Inside, the foyer opens to the dining room on the right and leads through a columned entrance to the great room with its warming fireplace and cathedral ceiling. The open kitchen easily serves the great room, the breakfast area and the dining room. A cathedral ceiling graces the master bedroom with its walk-in closet and private bath with a dual vanity and a whirlpool tub. Two additional bedrooms share a full bath. A detached garage with a skylit bonus room above is connected to the covered rear porch.

REAR EXTERIOR

plan# HPT910013

- STYLE: FARMHOUSE
- SQUARE FOOTAGE: 1,815
- BONUS SPACE: 336 SQ. FT.
- BEDROOMS: 3
- BATHROOMS: 2
- WIDTH: 70'-8"
- DEPTH: 70'-2"

SEARCH ONLINE @ EPLANS.COM

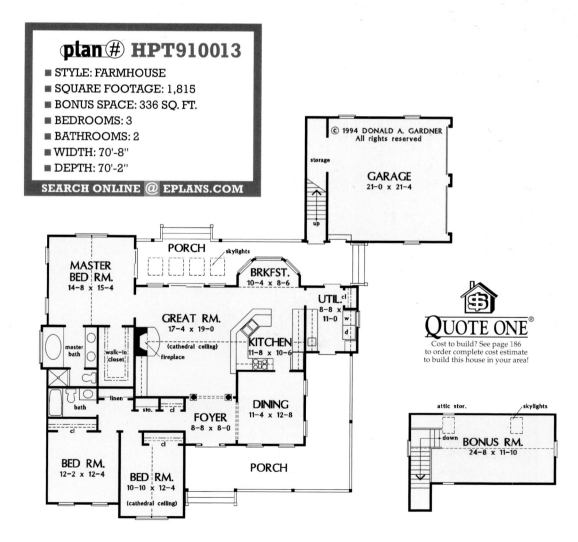

© 1994 DONALD A. GARDNER
All rights reserved

GARAGE
21-0 x 21-4

storage

PORCH

MASTER
BED RM.
14-8 x 15-4

BRKFST.
10-4 x 8-6

UTIL.
8-8 x
11-0

GREAT RM.
17-4 x 19-0
(cathedral ceiling)

KITCHEN
11-8 x 10-6

master
bath

walk-in
closet

fireplace

linen

bath

sto.

FOYER
8-8 x 8-0

DINING
11-4 x 12-8

BED RM.
12-2 x 12-4

BED RM.
10-10 x 12-4
(cathedral ceiling)

PORCH

QUOTE ONE®

Cost to build? See page 186
to order complete cost estimate
to build this house in your area!

attic stor.   skylights

down

BONUS RM.
24-8 x 11-10

This charming country plan boasts a cathedral ceiling in the great room. Dormer windows shed light on the foyer, which opens to a front bedroom/study and to the formal dining room. The kitchen is completely open to the great room and features a stylish snack-bar island and a bay window in the breakfast nook. The master suite offers a tray ceiling and a skylit bath. Two secondary bedrooms share a full bath on the opposite side of the house. Bonus space over the garage may be developed in the future.

plan# HPT910014

- STYLE: FARMHOUSE
- SQUARE FOOTAGE: 1,832
- BONUS SPACE: 425 SQ. FT.
- BEDROOMS: 3
- BATHROOMS: 2
- WIDTH: 65'-4"
- DEPTH: 62'-0"

SEARCH ONLINE @ EPLANS.COM

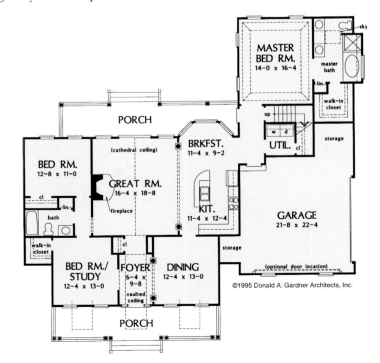

©1995 Donald A. Gardner Architects, Inc.

B. NATHAN

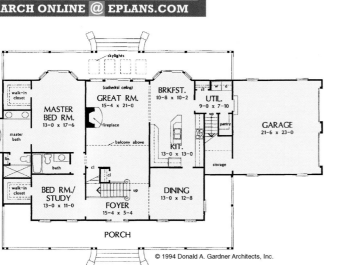

plan# HPT910015

- STYLE: FARMHOUSE
- FIRST FLOOR: 1,841 SQ. FT.
- SECOND FLOOR: 594 SQ. FT.
- TOTAL: 2,435 SQ. FT.
- BONUS SPACE: 391 SQ. FT.
- BEDROOMS: 4
- BATHROOMS: 3
- WIDTH: 82'-2"
- DEPTH: 48'-10"

SEARCH ONLINE @ EPLANS.COM

Spaciousness and lots of amenities earmark this design as a family favorite. The front wraparound porch leads to the foyer, where a bedroom/study and dining room open. The central great room presents a warming fireplace, a two-story cathedral ceiling and access to the rear porch. The kitchen features an island food-prep counter and opens to a bayed breakfast area, which conveniently accesses the garage through a side utility room. In the master suite, a private bath with a bumped-out tub and a walk-in closet are extra enhancements. Upstairs, two bedrooms flank a full bath. A bonus room over the garage allows for future expansion.

SECOND FLOOR

FIRST FLOOR

© 1994 Donald A. Gardner Architects, Inc.

This plan's wide front porch says "welcome home." Inside, its comfortable design encourages relaxation. A center dormer lights the foyer, as columns punctuate the entry to the dining room and the great room. The spacious kitchen offers an angled countertop and is open to the breakfast bay. A roomy utility area is nearby. Tray ceilings add elegance to the dining room and master bedroom. A possible second master suite is located opposite and features an optional arrangement for wheelchair accessibility. Two additional bedrooms share a third full bath that includes a linen closet.

plan# HPT910016

- STYLE: COUNTRY
- SQUARE FOOTAGE: 2,349
- BONUS SPACE: 435 SQ. FT.
- BEDROOMS: 4
- BATHROOMS: 3
- WIDTH: 83'-2"
- DEPTH: 56'-4"

SEARCH ONLINE @ EPLANS.COM

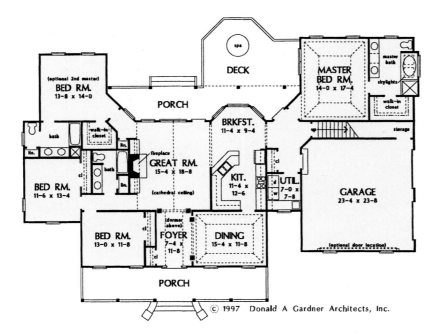

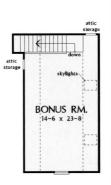

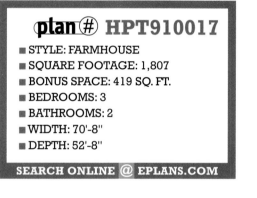

plan # HPT910017

- **STYLE: FARMHOUSE**
- **SQUARE FOOTAGE: 1,807**
- **BONUS SPACE: 419 SQ. FT.**
- **BEDROOMS: 3**
- **BATHROOMS: 2**
- **WIDTH: 70'-8"**
- **DEPTH: 52'-8"**

SEARCH ONLINE @ EPLANS.COM

This comfortable country home begins with a front porch that opens to a columned foyer. To the right, enter the formal dining room. Decorative columns define the central great room, which boasts wide views of the outdoors. A breakfast nook nearby accommodates casual dining. The master suite and the great room both open to the rear porch. Family bedrooms share a full bath that includes double lavatories. Stairs next to the two-car garage lead up to a skylit bonus room, which can be utilized as useful storage space.

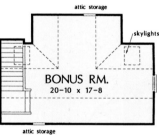

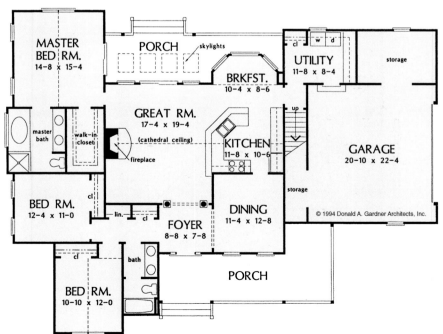

This lovely country home provides a powerful combination of well-defined formal rooms, casual living space and flexible areas. A foyer with a convenient coat closet leads to a spacious great room packed with amenities. Decorative columns announce the formal dining room, easily served by a gourmet kitchen, which boasts a breakfast area and bay window. The master bedroom offers a tray ceiling, a lovely triple window and a skylit bath. Bonus space above the garage features its own skylights and additional storage.

plan# HPT910018

- STYLE: COUNTRY
- SQUARE FOOTAGE: 1,685
- BONUS SPACE: 331 SQ. FT.
- BEDROOMS: 3
- BATHROOMS: 2
- WIDTH: 62'-4"
- DEPTH: 57'-4"

SEARCH ONLINE @ EPLANS.COM

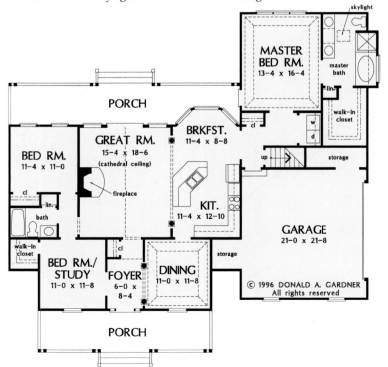

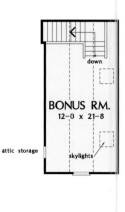

TO ORDER BLUEPRINTS CALL TOLL FREE 1-800-521-6797

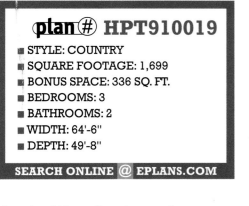

plan # HPT910019

- STYLE: COUNTRY
- SQUARE FOOTAGE: 1,699
- BONUS SPACE: 336 SQ. FT.
- BEDROOMS: 3
- BATHROOMS: 2
- WIDTH: 64'-6"
- DEPTH: 49'-8"

SEARCH ONLINE @ EPLANS.COM

An inviting front porch, dormers, gables and windows topped by half-rounds give this home curb appeal. Inside, an open floor plan with a split-bedroom design and a spacious bonus room steal the show. Two dormers add light and volume to the foyer; a cathedral ceiling enlarges the open great room. Accent columns define the foyer, great room, kitchen and breakfast area. Both the dining room and the front bedroom/study have tray ceilings that show off stunning picture windows with half-rounds. The private master suite with a tray ceiling accesses the rear deck through sliding glass doors, and the bath includes a garden tub, separate shower and two skylights over a double-bowl vanity.

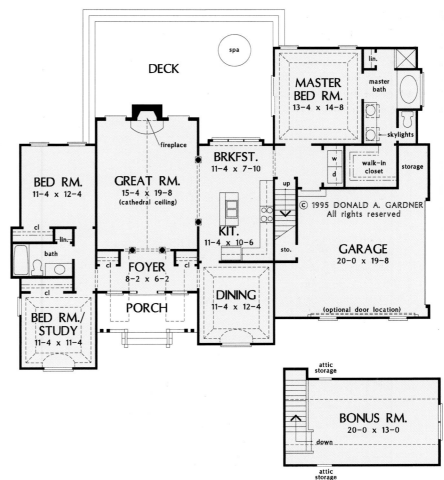

© 2001 Donald A. Gardner, Inc.

A triplet of dormers, two box-bay windows and a skylit rear porch ensure that this home will have plenty of natural illumination. Tray ceilings highlight the dining room, bedroom/study and master bedroom, while the great room displays a vaulted ceiling. The breakfast area, sunlit through its wall of windows, shares a snack bar with the kitchen. The split-bedroom floor plan, with the master suite to the left and secondary bedrooms to the right, allows privacy for all family members. A spacious bonus room resides above the garage.

plan# HPT910020

- STYLE: COUNTRY
- SQUARE FOOTAGE: 2,038
- BONUS SPACE: 365 SQ. FT.
- BEDROOMS: 4
- BATHROOMS: 3
- WIDTH: 68'-0"
- DEPTH: 54'-4"

SEARCH ONLINE @ EPLANS.COM

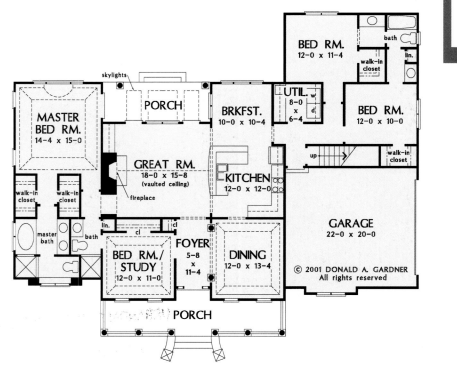

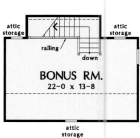

© 2001 Donald A. Gardner, Inc

plan # HPT910021

- **STYLE:** COUNTRY
- **SQUARE FOOTAGE:** 2,413
- **BONUS SPACE:** 417 SQ. FT.
- **BEDROOMS:** 4
- **BATHROOMS:** 2½
- **WIDTH:** 78'-8"
- **DEPTH:** 57'-8"

SEARCH ONLINE @ EPLANS.COM

Dormers set above a charming porch and beautiful entry door with arched transoms lend eye appeal to this wonderful four-bedroom design. The foyer leads to the dining room to the right and a bedroom or study to the left—both feature exciting ceiling treatments. The hearth-warmed great room shares an open area with the island kitchen and bayed breakfast nook. The master suite enjoys plenty of privacy, tucked to the rear of the garage. The master bath includes a tub set in a corner window and a walk-in closet. Two family bedrooms sharing a full bath reside to the left of the plan.

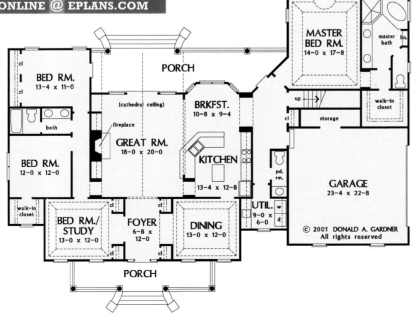

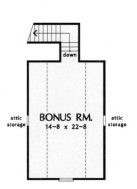

© 1999 Donald A. Gardner, Inc.

A trio of dormers and an inviting front porch create a classic country exterior for this four-bedroom home. At the heart of the home is a marvelous great room with a cathedral ceiling and built-in bookcases bordering the fireplace. The great room is open to the kitchen and bay-windowed breakfast room. A generous back porch extends living space to the outdoors. A split-bedroom design provides privacy for the master suite with a tray ceiling, walk-in closet, and luxurious bath. Three additional bedrooms, one with a cathedral ceiling, walk-in closet and private bath, are positioned on the opposite side of the home.

plan # HPT910022

- STYLE: COUNTRY
- SQUARE FOOTAGE: 2,195
- BONUS SPACE: 556 SQ. FT.
- BEDROOMS: 4
- BATHROOMS: 3
- WIDTH: 71'-8"
- DEPTH: 54'-4"

SEARCH ONLINE @ EPLANS.COM

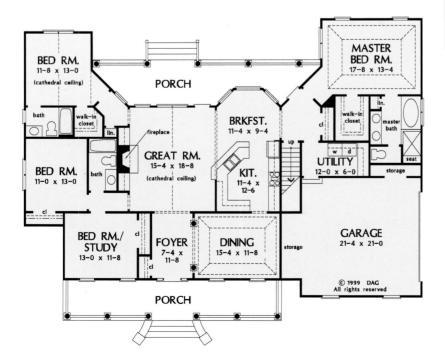

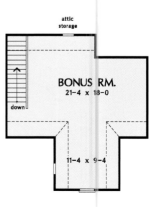

B. NATHAN

plan # HPT910023

- **STYLE:** COUNTRY
- **SQUARE FOOTAGE:** 2,273
- **BONUS SPACE:** 342 SQ. FT.
- **BEDROOMS:** 4
- **BATHROOMS:** 2½
- **WIDTH:** 74'-8"
- **DEPTH:** 75'-10"

SEARCH ONLINE @ EPLANS.COM

With an exciting blend of styles, this home features the wrapping porch of a country farmhouse with a brick-and-siding exterior for a uniquely pleasing effect. The great room shares its cathedral ceiling with an open kitchen, while the octagonal dining room is complemented by a tray ceiling. Built-ins flank the great room's fireplace for added convenience. The master suite features a full bath, a walk-in closet and access to the rear porch. Two additional bedrooms share a full hall bath; a third bedroom can be converted into a study. Skylit bonus space is available above the garage, which is connected to the home by a covered breezeway.

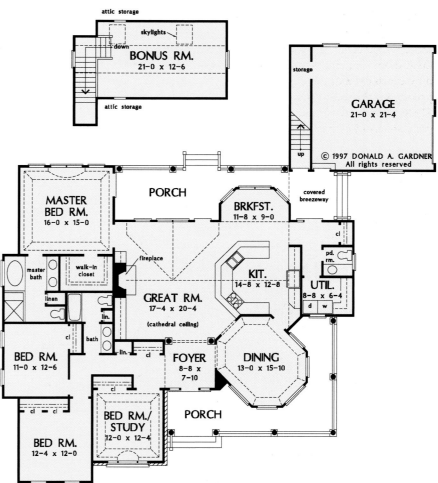

© 1998 Donald A. Gardner, Inc.

A trio of dormers and a front porch adorn the facade of this sprawling four-bedroom country home. Illuminated by the center dormer, the vaulted foyer gives way to the dining room with a tray ceiling and the spacious great room with a cathedral ceiling, a fireplace and built-in shelves. A split-bedroom layout provides privacy for homeowners in a generous master suite with a tray ceiling and private bath. Three additional bedrooms reside on the opposite side of the home.

plan# HPT910024

- **STYLE: COUNTRY**
- **SQUARE FOOTAGE: 2,487**
- **BEDROOMS: 4**
- **BATHROOMS: 3**
- **WIDTH: 86'-2"**
- **DEPTH: 51'-8"**

SEARCH ONLINE @ EPLANS.COM

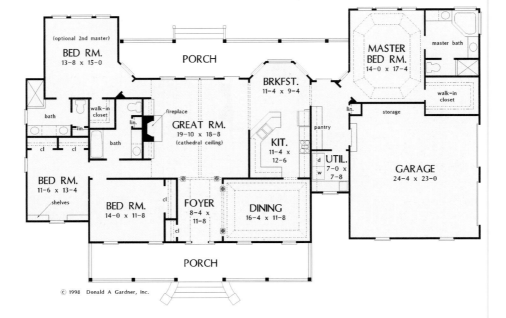

© 1998 Donald A Gardner, Inc.

plan # HPT910025

- **STYLE: FARMHOUSE**
- **SQUARE FOOTAGE: 1,346**
- **BEDROOMS: 3**
- **BATHROOMS: 2**
- **WIDTH: 65'-0"**
- **DEPTH: 44'-2"**

SEARCH ONLINE @ EPLANS.COM

A great room that stretches into the dining room makes this design perfect for entertaining. A cozy fireplace, stylish built-ins and a cathedral ceiling further this casual yet elegant atmosphere. A rear deck extends living possibilities. The ample kitchen features an abundance of counter and cabinet space and an angled cooktop and serving bar that overlooks the great room. Two bedrooms, a hall bath and a handy laundry room make up the family sleeping wing; the master suite is privately located at the rear of the plan.

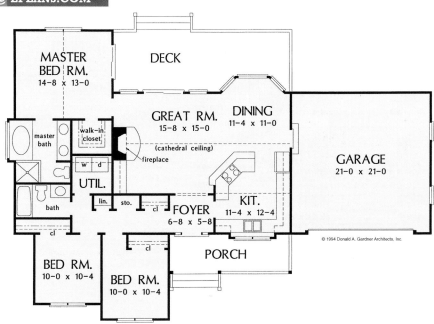

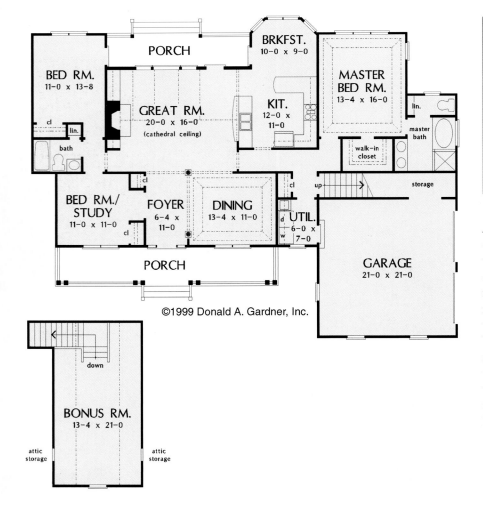

PORCH

BRKFST.
10-0 x 9-0

BED RM.
11-0 x 13-8

MASTER
BED RM.
13-4 x 16-0

lin.

GREAT RM.
20-0 x 16-0
(cathedral ceiling)

KIT.
12-0 x
11-0

master
bath

cl

lin.

bath

walk-in
closet

cl

cl

up

storage

BED RM./
STUDY
11-0 x 11-0

FOYER
6-4 x
11-0

DINING
13-4 x 11-0

cl

UTIL.
6-0 x
7-0

d

w

cl

PORCH

GARAGE
21-0 x 21-0

©1999 Donald A. Gardner, Inc.

down

BONUS RM.
13-4 x 21-0

attic
storage

attic
storage

plan # HPT910026

- **STYLE: COUNTRY**
- **SQUARE FOOTAGE: 1,733**
- **BONUS SPACE: 372 SQ. FT.**
- **BEDROOMS: 3**
- **BATHROOMS: 2**
- **WIDTH: 65'-8"**
- **DEPTH: 49'-8"**

SEARCH ONLINE @ EPLANS.COM

A trio of dormers with arch-top windows and a country porch adorn the facade of this gracious three-bedroom home. Columns and a tray ceiling grant distinction and definition to the formal dining room; the great room is enriched by a cathedral ceiling with two rear clerestory dormers, a fireplace and built-in bookshelves. The home's split-bedroom design provides plenty of privacy for the master suite, which features a tray ceiling, walk-in closet and bath. Two secondary bedrooms, one with back-porch access, share a hall bath with a linen closet.

plan# HPT910027

- STYLE: COUNTRY
- SQUARE FOOTAGE: 1,498
- BEDROOMS: 3
- BATHROOMS: 2
- WIDTH: 59'-8"
- DEPTH: 46'-8"

SEARCH ONLINE @ EPLANS.COM

This charming country home utilizes multi-pane windows, columns, dormers and a covered porch to offer a welcoming front exterior. Inside, the great room with a dramatic cathedral ceiling commands attention; the kitchen and breakfast room are just beyond a set of columns. The tray-ceilinged dining room presents a delightfully formal atmosphere for dinner parties or family gatherings. A tray ceiling in the master bedroom contributes to its pleasant atmosphere, as do the large walk-in closet and the gracious private bath with a garden tub and a separate shower. The secondary bedrooms are located at the opposite end of the house for privacy.

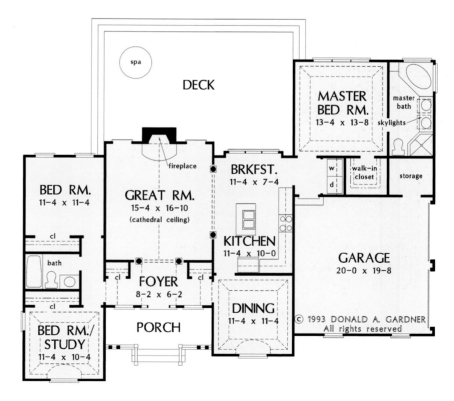

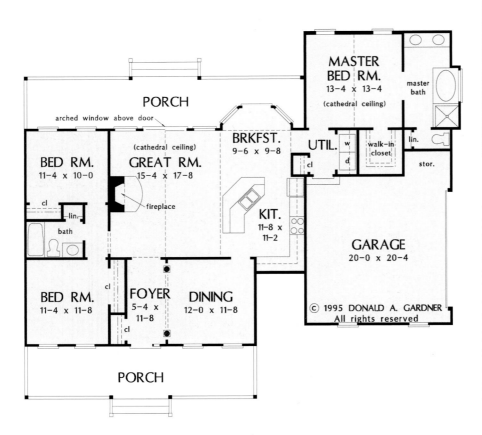

plan # HPT910028

- **STYLE:** FARMHOUSE
- **SQUARE FOOTAGE:** 1,561
- **BEDROOMS:** 3
- **BATHROOMS:** 2
- **WIDTH:** 60'-10"
- **DEPTH:** 51'-6"

SEARCH ONLINE @ EPLANS.COM

Combining the finest country details with the most modern livability, this one-story home makes modest budgets really stretch. The welcoming front porch encourages you to stop and enjoy the summer breezes. The entry foyer leads to a formal dining room defined by columns. Beyond is the large great room with a cathedral ceiling and a fireplace. The kitchen and the breakfast room are open to the living area and include porch access. The master suite is tucked away in its own private space. It is conveniently separated from the family bedrooms, which share a full bath. The two-car garage contains extra storage space.

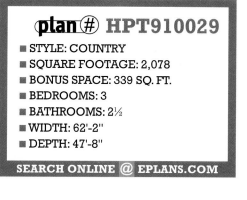

plan# HPT910029

- STYLE: COUNTRY
- SQUARE FOOTAGE: 2,078
- BONUS SPACE: 339 SQ. FT.
- BEDROOMS: 3
- BATHROOMS: 2½
- WIDTH: 62'-2"
- DEPTH: 47'-8"

SEARCH ONLINE @ EPLANS.COM

An enchanting L-shaped front porch lends charm and grace to this country home with dual dormers and gables. Bay windows expand both of the home's dining areas; the great room and kitchen are amplified by a shared cathedral ceiling. The generous great room features a fireplace with flanking built-ins, skylights and access to a marvelous back porch. A cathedral ceiling enhances the master suite, which enjoys a large walk-in closet and a luxurious bath. Two more bedrooms share a generous hall bath that has a dual-sink vanity.

©1999 Donald A. Gardner, Inc.

This compact design has all the amenities available in larger plans with little wasted space. In addition, a wraparound covered porch, a front Palladian window, dormers and rear arched windows provide exciting visual elements to the exterior. The spacious great room has a fireplace, a cathedral ceiling and clerestory windows. A second-level balcony overlooks this gathering area. The kitchen is centrally located for maximum flexibility in layout and features a pass-through to the great room. Besides the generous first-floor master suite with a pampering bath, two family bedrooms located on the second level share a full bath.

plan# HPT910030
- STYLE: FARMHOUSE
- FIRST FLOOR: 1,325 SQ. FT.
- SECOND FLOOR: 453 SQ. FT.
- TOTAL: 1,778 SQ. FT.
- BEDROOMS: 3
- BATHROOMS: 2½
- WIDTH: 48'-4"
- DEPTH: 51'-10"

SEARCH ONLINE @ EPLANS.COM

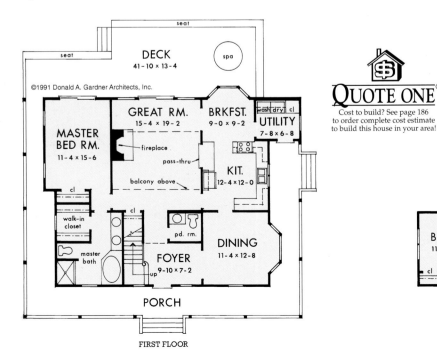

QUOTE ONE®
Cost to build? See page 186
to order complete cost estimate
to build this house in your area!

©1991 Donald A. Gardner Architects, Inc.

DECK
41-10 × 13-4

seat

spa

seat

GREAT RM.
15-4 × 19-2

BRKFST.
9-0 × 9-2

wash dry cl

UTILITY
7-8 × 6-8

MASTER
BED RM.
11-4 × 15-6

fireplace

pass-thru

KIT.
12-4 × 12-0

balcony above

cl

walk-in
closet

cl

pd. rm.

DINING
11-4 × 12-8

master
bath

FOYER
9-10 × 7-2

up

PORCH

FIRST FLOOR

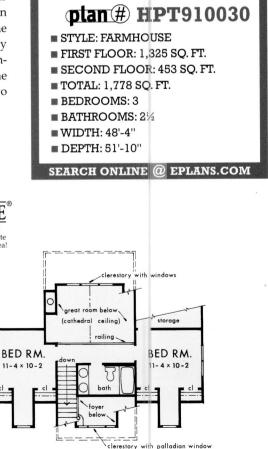

clerestory with windows

great room below
(cathedral ceiling)

storage

railing

BED RM.
11-4 × 10-2

down

BED RM.
11-4 × 10-2

cl

cl

bath

cl

foyer
below

clerestory with palladian window

SECOND FLOOR

plan# HPT910031

- STYLE: FARMHOUSE
- FIRST FLOOR: 1,618 SQ. FT.
- SECOND FLOOR: 570 SQ. FT.
- TOTAL: 2,188 SQ. FT.
- BONUS SPACE: 495 SQ. FT.
- BEDROOMS: 3
- BATHROOMS: 2½
- WIDTH: 87'-0"
- DEPTH: 57'-0"

SEARCH ONLINE @ EPLANS.COM

QUOTE ONE®
Cost to build? See page 186 to order complete cost estimate to build this house in your area!

The entrance foyer and great room with sloped ceilings have Palladian window clerestories that allow natural light to enter this charming farmhouse. All other first-floor spaces have nine-foot ceilings. The spacious great room boasts a fireplace, cabinets and bookshelves. The second-floor balcony overlooks the great room. The kitchen with a cooking island is conveniently located between the dining room and the breakfast room with an open view of the great room. A generous master bedroom has plenty of closet space as well as an expansive master bath. A bonus room over the garage allows for expansion.

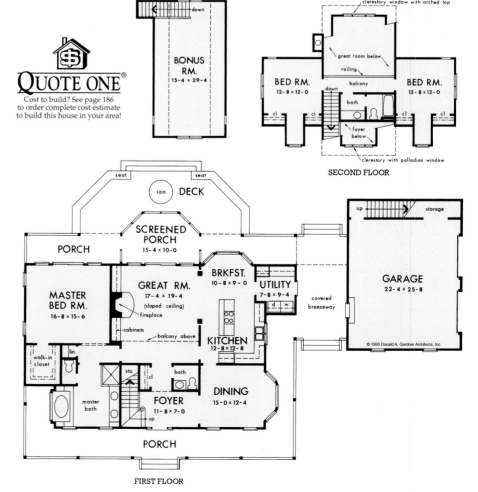

FIRST FLOOR

© 2001 Donald A. Gardner, Inc.

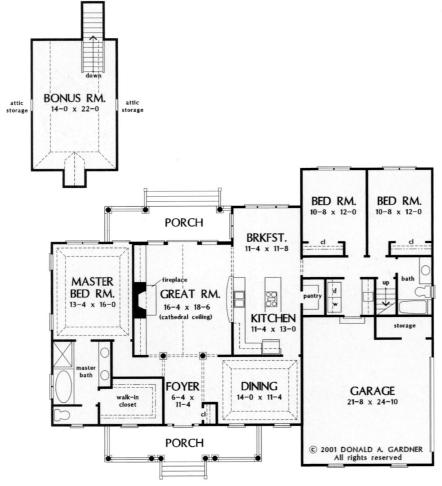

BONUS RM.
14-0 x 22-0

attic storage   attic storage

down

PORCH

MASTER BED RM.
13-4 x 16-0

fireplace

GREAT RM.
16-4 x 18-6
(cathedral ceiling)

BRKFST.
11-4 x 11-8

KITCHEN
11-4 x 13-0

BED RM.
10-8 x 12-0

BED RM.
10-8 x 12-0

cl   cl

pantry

bath

up

storage

master bath

walk-in closet

FOYER
6-4 x 11-4

DINING
14-0 x 11-4

GARAGE
21-8 x 24-10

PORCH

plan# HPT910032

- STYLE: COUNTRY
- SQUARE FOOTAGE: 1,915
- BONUS SPACE: 364 SQ. FT.
- BEDROOMS: 3
- BATHROOMS: 2
- WIDTH: 64'-4"
- DEPTH: 50'-2"

SEARCH ONLINE @ EPLANS.COM

Don't overlook this home's country flair. With open yet definable rooms, this classic has been updated for easier living. Sidelights and clerestories welcome light, as columns and a pass-through replace sections of walls to allow a brighter, more open home. While pantry and closet space is abundant, decorative ceiling treatments visually expand rooms such as the master bedroom. Two additional bedrooms share a bath and are ideally located next to the utility area and bonus-room staircase. The master suite features a bath with a spacious shower and enjoys rear-porch access.

© 1997 Donald A. Gardner Architects, Inc.

plan# HPT910033

- **STYLE: COUNTRY**
- **FIRST FLOOR: 1,743 SQ. FT.**
- **SECOND FLOOR: 555 SQ. FT.**
- **TOTAL: 2,298 SQ. FT.**
- **BONUS SPACE: 350 SQ. FT.**
- **BEDROOMS: 4**
- **BATHROOMS: 3**
- **WIDTH: 77'-11"**
- **DEPTH: 53'-2"**

SEARCH ONLINE @ EPLANS.COM

A lovely arch-top window and a wraparound porch set off this country exterior. Inside, formal rooms open off the foyer, which leads to a spacious great room. This living area provides a fireplace and access to a screened porch with a cathedral ceiling. Bay windows allow natural light into the breakfast area and formal dining room. The master suite features a spacious bath and access to a private area of the rear porch. Two second-floor bedrooms share a bath and a balcony hall that offers an overlook to the great room.

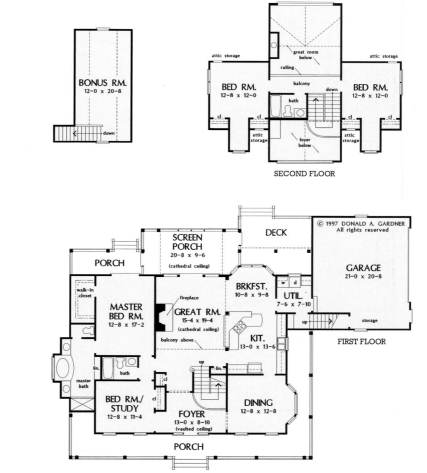

COUNTRY/FARMHOUSE DESIGNS

© 1997 Donald A. Gardner Architects, Inc.

A classic country exterior enriches the appearance of this economical home, and its front porch and two skylit back porches encourage weekend relaxation. The great room features a cathedral ceiling and a fireplace with adjacent built-ins. The master suite enjoys a double-door entry, back-porch access and a tray ceiling. The master bath has a garden tub set in the corner, a separate shower, twin vanities and a skylight. Loads of storage, an open floor plan and walls of windows make this three-bedroom plan very livable.

plan# HPT910034

- STYLE: COUNTRY
- SQUARE FOOTAGE: 1,652
- BONUS SPACE: 367 SQ. FT.
- BEDROOMS: 3
- BATHROOMS: 2
- WIDTH: 64'-4"
- DEPTH: 51'-0"

SEARCH ONLINE @ EPLANS.COM

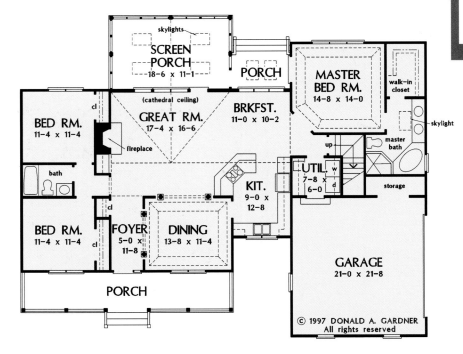

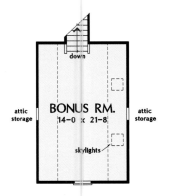

© 2000 Donald A. Gardner, Inc.

plan# HPT910035

- **STYLE: COUNTRY**
- **FIRST FLOOR: 1,437 SQ. FT.**
- **SECOND FLOOR: 531 SQ. FT.**
- **TOTAL: 1,968 SQ. FT.**
- **BEDROOMS: 3**
- **BATHROOMS: 2½**
- **WIDTH: 51'-4"**
- **DEPTH: 41'-6"**

SEARCH ONLINE @ EPLANS.COM

This sophisticated country home is economical and cozy, yet it has all the amenities of a larger plan. From the wraparound porch to the vaulted great room, this floor plan provides space for family togetherness, as well as personal privacy. The secluded master suite contains two spacious walk-in closets, double lavatories and a garden tub. Another incredible feature is the large master shower. Upstairs, a full bath and impressive balcony view separate the two bedrooms. Bay windows highlight the breakfast nook and dining room, while the central dormer floods the foyer with light. Other special features include the kitchen's angled countertop—complementing an open floor plan in the family areas.

SECOND FLOOR

FIRST FLOOR

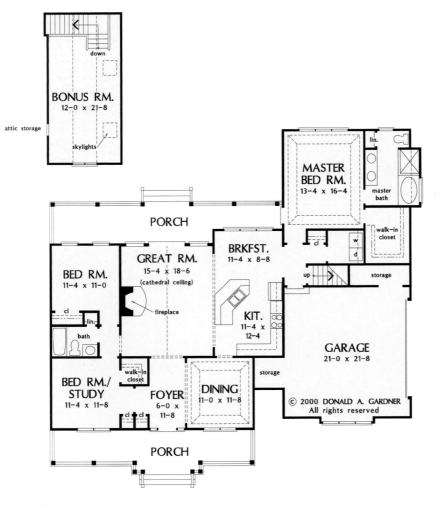

plan# HPT910036

- STYLE: COUNTRY
- SQUARE FOOTAGE: 1,724
- BONUS SPACE: 329 SQ. FT.
- BEDROOMS: 3
- BATHROOMS: 2
- WIDTH: 62'-4"
- DEPTH: 57'-10"

SEARCH ONLINE @ EPLANS.COM

Stylish and sensible, this modestly sized home makes the most of its square footage and is ready for expansion with a skylit bonus room. Taking the floor plan to new heights is a cathedral ceiling in the great room and tray ceilings in both the dining room and master bedroom. Triplet windows are fashionable additions to the breakfast area and master bedroom, and a box-bay window adds a special touch to the garage. The foyer opens to the great room and dining room, for effortless gatherings. A full-size bath is strategically located for easy accessibility from any part of the home. The master suite is a haven, complete with a spacious walk-in closet, His and Her lavatories, a garden tub, and large shower.

© 2002 Donald A. Gardner, Inc.

plan # HPT910037

- STYLE: COUNTRY
- SQUARE FOOTAGE: 2,037
- BONUS SPACE: 361 SQ. FT.
- BEDROOMS: 3
- BATHROOMS: 2½
- WIDTH: 62'-4"
- DEPTH: 61'-8"

SEARCH ONLINE @ EPLANS.COM

Horizontal siding and a wide front porch establish the country character of this design. Inside, the dining room to the right of the foyer features a tray ceiling; a bedroom/study to the left of the foyer includes a long wall closet and shares a full bath with another bedroom. A cathedral ceiling, fireplace and access to the rear porch enrich the central great room. Illuminated by a bay window, the expansive kitchen/breakfast area provides an informal dining spot. The master bedroom, with a tray ceiling, spacious walk-in closet and private bath, sits to the rear of the plan. A bonus room above the garage is the perfect spot for a recreation or game room.

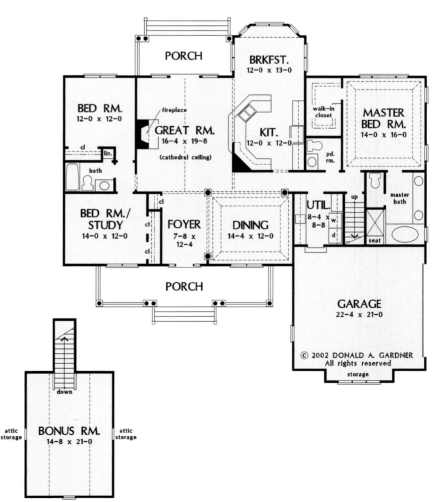

© 2002 DONALD A. GARDNER
All rights reserved

Twin gables and a generous front porch give this graceful farmhouse stature and appeal. A rear deck adds outdoor expansion to the great room, which features a fireplace, built-ins, a convenient rear staircase and an overlooking balcony. The first-floor master suite enjoys His and Hers walk-in closets and a private bath with a garden tub. A versatile bedroom/study and full bath are nearby. Located upstairs are two family bedrooms, a loft with built-in bookshelves, an ample second-floor bath and a bonus room.

plan# HPT910038

- STYLE: FARMHOUSE
- FIRST FLOOR: 1,718 SQ. FT.
- SECOND FLOOR: 638 SQ. FT.
- TOTAL: 2,356 SQ. FT.
- BONUS SPACE: 348 SQ. FT.
- BEDROOMS: 4
- BATHROOMS: 3
- WIDTH: 71'-0"
- DEPTH: 42'-8"

SEARCH ONLINE @ EPLANS.COM

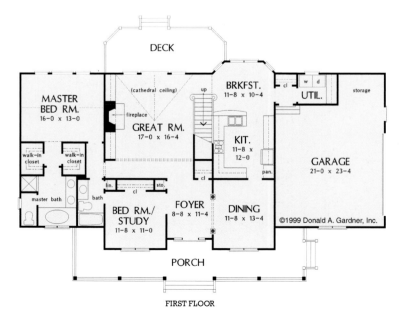

FIRST FLOOR

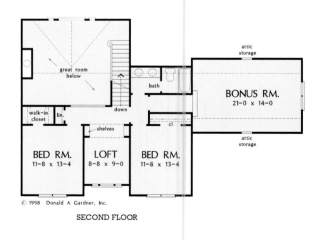

SECOND FLOOR

plan # HPT910039

- **STYLE: FARMHOUSE**
- **FIRST FLOOR: 1,580 SQ. FT.**
- **SECOND FLOOR: 526 SQ. FT.**
- **TOTAL: 2,106 SQ. FT.**
- **BONUS SPACE: 225 SQ. FT.**
- **BEDROOMS: 3**
- **BATHROOMS: 2½**
- **WIDTH: 49'-8"**
- **DEPTH: 59'-5"**

SEARCH ONLINE @ EPLANS.COM

Comfort is highlighted throughout this country home. Flanking the foyer are a study and a formal dining room. The great room enjoys a two-story ceiling along with a cozy fireplace and access to the rear porch— great for family gatherings! The eloquent master bedroom boasts a vaulted ceiling, which gives an aura of spaciousness, and enjoys a large walk-in closet and a pampering private bath with an oversized bayed tub. The second floor holds two additional bedrooms, a full bath and a bonus room.

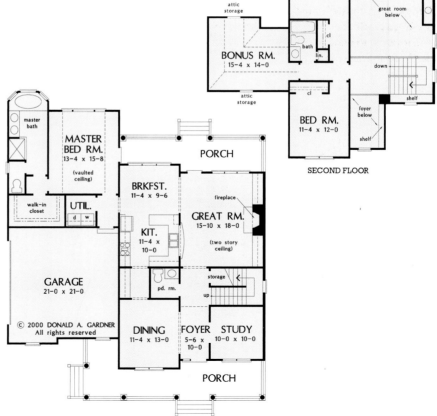

SECOND FLOOR

FIRST FLOOR

Two symmetrical bay windows accent the formal living and dining rooms of this design. The foyer leads straight back to the family room and rear porch. A fireplace, built-ins and an overhead balcony grace the family room. Between the dining room and kitchen, there's a handy pantry area. The utility room and a powder room are to the right of the breakfast room. The master suite is off the family room and includes a walk-in closet and a bath with a double-bowl vanity. Upstairs, three bedrooms share a hall bath and a loft/study that overlooks the family room.

plan# HPT910040

- STYLE: FARMHOUSE
- FIRST FLOOR: 1,943 SQ. FT.
- SECOND FLOOR: 1,000 SQ. FT.
- TOTAL: 2,943 SQ. FT.
- BONUS SPACE: 403 SQ. FT.
- BEDROOMS: 4
- BATHROOMS: 2½
- WIDTH: 79'-10"
- DEPTH: 51'-8"

SEARCH ONLINE @ EPLANS.COM

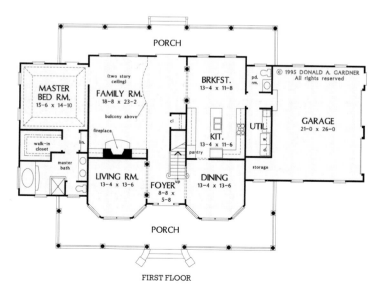

FIRST FLOOR

SECOND FLOOR

TO ORDER BLUEPRINTS CALL TOLL FREE 1-800-521-6797

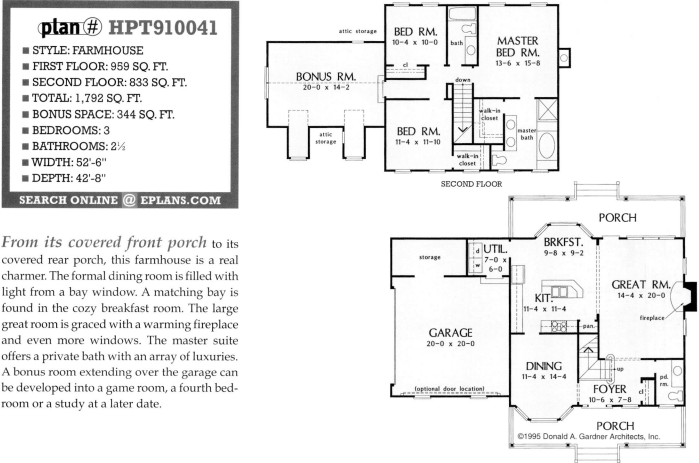

plan # HPT910041

- STYLE: FARMHOUSE
- FIRST FLOOR: 959 SQ. FT.
- SECOND FLOOR: 833 SQ. FT.
- TOTAL: 1,792 SQ. FT.
- BONUS SPACE: 344 SQ. FT.
- BEDROOMS: 3
- BATHROOMS: 2½
- WIDTH: 52'-6"
- DEPTH: 42'-8"

SEARCH ONLINE @ EPLANS.COM

From its covered front porch to its covered rear porch, this farmhouse is a real charmer. The formal dining room is filled with light from a bay window. A matching bay is found in the cozy breakfast room. The large great room is graced with a warming fireplace and even more windows. The master suite offers a private bath with an array of luxuries. A bonus room extending over the garage can be developed into a game room, a fourth bedroom or a study at a later date.

SECOND FLOOR

FIRST FLOOR

©1995 Donald A. Gardner Architects, Inc.

At the front of this farmhouse design, the master suite includes a sitting bay, two walk-in closets, a door to the front porch and a compartmented bath with a double-bowl vanity. The formal dining room in the second bay also features a door to the front porch. Access the rear porch from the great room, which is open to the breakfast room under the balcony. On the second floor, three family bedrooms share a bath that has a double-bowl vanity. One of the family bedrooms offers a walk-in closet. A bonus room over the garage can be used as a study or game room.

plan # HPT910042

- STYLE: FARMHOUSE
- FIRST FLOOR: 1,614 SQ. FT.
- SECOND FLOOR: 892 SQ. FT.
- TOTAL: 2,506 SQ. FT.
- BONUS SPACE: 341 SQ. FT.
- BEDROOMS: 4
- BATHROOMS: 2½
- WIDTH: 71'-10"
- DEPTH: 50'-0"

SEARCH ONLINE @ EPLANS.COM

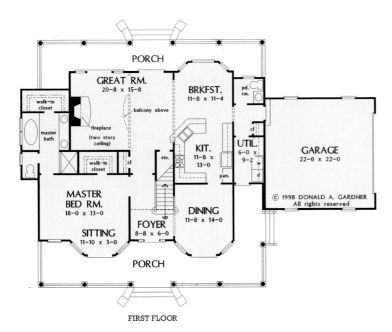

FIRST FLOOR

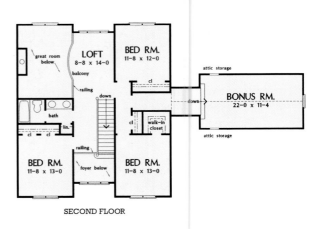

SECOND FLOOR

TO ORDER BLUEPRINTS CALL TOLL FREE 1-800-521-6797

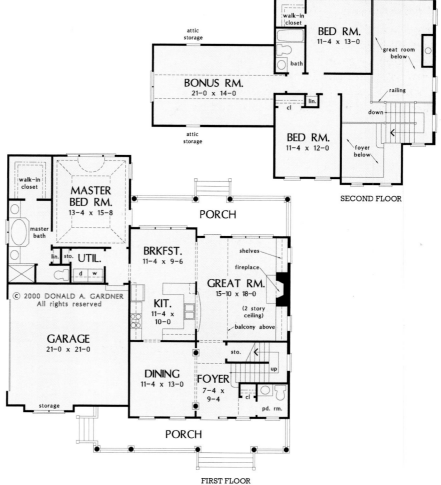

plan# HPT910043

- **STYLE: FARMHOUSE**
- **FIRST FLOOR: 1,412 SQ. FT.**
- **SECOND FLOOR: 506 SQ. FT.**
- **TOTAL: 1,918 SQ. FT.**
- **BONUS SPACE: 320 SQ. FT.**
- **BEDROOMS: 3**
- **BATHROOMS: 2½**
- **WIDTH: 49'-8"**
- **DEPTH: 52'-0"**

SEARCH ONLINE @ EPLANS.COM

Here's a country home with plenty of open interior space. Just off the foyer, a powder room and coat closet are thoughtfully placed to accommodate guests. A fireplace and built-ins highlight the great room. A formal dining room adjoins the kitchen and breakfast area, which features a triple window. Wrapping counter space in the kitchen provides enough food-preparation space for two cooks. The master suite includes a walk-in closet, well-appointed bath and additional linen storage. Upstairs, two family bedrooms share a hall bath and access to a spacious bonus room.

© 1996 Donald A. Gardner Architects, Inc.

B. NATHAN.

MASTER BED RM.
16-2 x 14-0

skylight

master bath

lin.

walk-in closets

cl

down

BED RM.
11-10 x 11-0

cl

bath

lin.

cl

BED RM.
11-10 x 11-2

railing

BED RM.
11-10 x 11-2

attic storage

down

skylights

BONUS RM.
21-4 x 15-8

attic storage

SECOND FLOOR

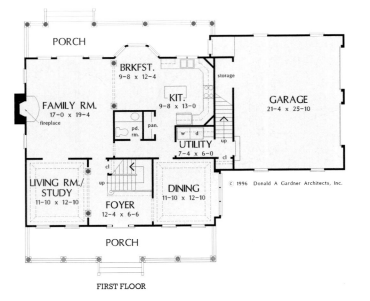

PORCH

BRKFST.
9-8 x 12-4

storage

FAMILY RM.
17-0 x 19-4
fireplace

KIT.
9-8 x 13-0

GARAGE
21-4 x 25-10

pd. rm.

pan.

w d

UTILITY
7-4 x 6-0

up

cl

© 1996   Donald A Gardner Architects, Inc.

LIVING RM./ STUDY
11-10 x 12-10

up

cl

DINING
11-10 x 12-10

FOYER
12-4 x 6-6

PORCH

FIRST FLOOR

plan # HPT910044

- STYLE: FARMHOUSE
- FIRST FLOOR: 1,299 SQ. FT.
- SECOND FLOOR: 1,176 SQ. FT.
- TOTAL: 2,475 SQ. FT.
- BONUS SPACE: 464 SQ. FT.
- BEDROOMS: 4
- BATHROOMS: 2½
- WIDTH: 64'-8"
- DEPTH: 47'-2"

SEARCH ONLINE @ EPLANS.COM

A large center gable with a Palladian window and a gently vaulted portico make this two-story home stand out from the typical farmhouse. A formal dining room and a living room/study, both highlighted by tray ceilings, flank the foyer, which leads into a spacious family room. Nine-foot ceilings add volume to the entire first floor, including the efficient kitchen with a center work island and large pantry. Upstairs, the gracious master suite features a tray ceiling, a generous walk-in closet, and a skylit bath with a double-bowl vanity, linen closet and garden tub. Three additional bedrooms share a full bath.

TO ORDER BLUEPRINTS CALL TOLL FREE 1-800-521-6797

© 2002 Donald A. Gardner, Inc.

plan # HPT910045

- STYLE: COUNTRY
- FIRST FLOOR: 1,420 SQ. FT.
- SECOND FLOOR: 1,065 SQ. FT.
- TOTAL: 2,485 SQ. FT.
- BONUS SPACE: 411 SQ. FT.
- BEDROOMS: 4
- BATHROOMS: 3
- WIDTH: 57'-8"
- DEPTH: 49'-0"

SEARCH ONLINE @ EPLANS.COM

Four dormers ornament the facade of this charming two-story country home. Tall windows in the dining room and bedroom/study overlook the front porch, while a wall of windows in the great room views the rear porch. A fireplace flanked by built-in shelves provides a focal point for the great room, which shares a snack bar with the kitchen. A butler's pantry leads from the kitchen to the dining room, providing discreet service for formal occasions. Upstairs, the master suite and two family bedrooms all feature walk-in closets; the master suite also includes a lavish bath with a shower that has a built-in seat. Two cozy dormer alcoves in the bonus room provide a quiet spot.

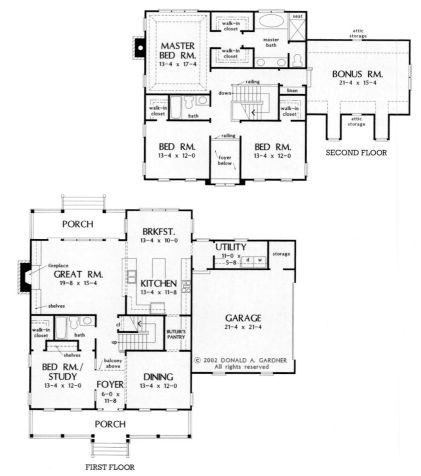

© 2001 Donald A. Gardner, Inc.

Country accents and farmhouse style enhance the facade of this lovely two-story home. The first floor provides a formal dining room and great room warmed by a fireplace. The kitchen connects to a breakfast bay — perfect for casual morning meals. The first-floor master suite includes two walk-in closets and a private bath. Upstairs, a loft overlooks the two-story great room. Three second-floor bedrooms share a hall bath. The bonus room above the garage is great for a home office or guest suite.

plan # HPT910046

- **STYLE: FARMHOUSE**
- **FIRST FLOOR: 1,667 SQ. FT.**
- **SECOND FLOOR: 803 SQ. FT.**
- **TOTAL: 2,470 SQ. FT.**
- **BONUS SPACE: 318 SQ. FT.**
- **BEDROOMS: 4**
- **BATHROOMS: 2½**
- **WIDTH: 52'-4"**
- **DEPTH: 57'-0"**

SEARCH ONLINE @ EPLANS.COM

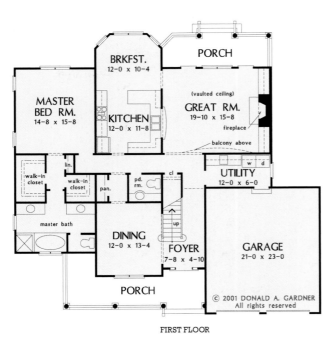

FIRST FLOOR

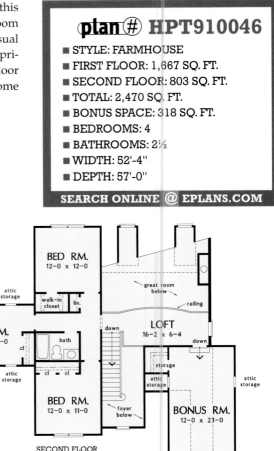

SECOND FLOOR

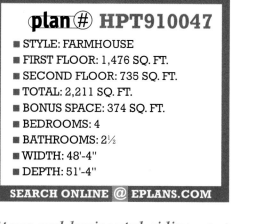

plan # HPT910047

- STYLE: FARMHOUSE
- FIRST FLOOR: 1,476 SQ. FT.
- SECOND FLOOR: 735 SQ. FT.
- TOTAL: 2,211 SQ. FT.
- BONUS SPACE: 374 SQ. FT.
- BEDROOMS: 4
- BATHROOMS: 2½
- WIDTH: 48'-4"
- DEPTH: 51'-4"

SEARCH ONLINE @ EPLANS.COM

Stone and horizontal siding paired with the covered front entry creates true country flavor for this four-bedroom home. The two-story foyer opens to the dining room on the left and the great room, where a warming fireplace adds to the country atmosphere. Views are offered in the great room and the breakfast nook that adjoins the kitchen. The master suite finds privacy on the first floor while three additional bedrooms are on the second floor, along with a sizable bonus room.

© 2002 Donald A. Gardner, Inc.

With spacious front and rear porches, twin gables and an arched entrance, this home has overwhelming charm and curb appeal. Columns make a grand impression both inside and outside, and transoms above French doors brighten both the front and rear of the floor plan. An angled counter separates the kitchen from the great room and breakfast area, and the mud room/utility area is complete with a sink. A tray ceiling tops the master bedroom. The formal living room/study and bonus room are flexible spaces, tailoring to family needs. A balcony overlooks the foyer and great room. An additional upstairs bedroom has its own bath and can be used as a guest suite.

plan ⊕ HPT910048

- STYLE: FARMHOUSE
- FIRST FLOOR: 1,798 SQ. FT.
- SECOND FLOOR: 723 SQ. FT.
- TOTAL: 2,521 SQ. FT.
- BONUS SPACE: 349 SQ. FT.
- BEDROOMS: 4
- BATHROOMS: 3½
- WIDTH: 66'-8"
- DEPTH: 49'-8"

SEARCH ONLINE @ EPLANS.COM

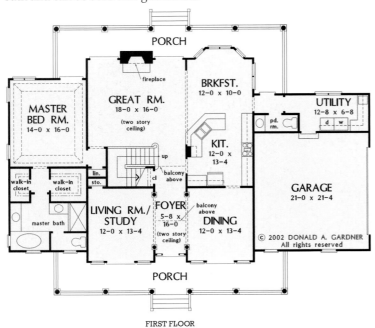

FIRST FLOOR

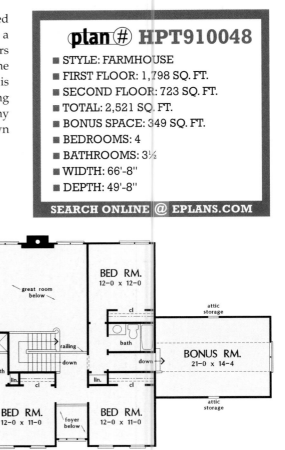

SECOND FLOOR

© 2001 Donald A. Gardner, Inc.

plan# HPT910049

- STYLE: FARMHOUSE
- FIRST FLOOR: 2,194 SQ. FT.
- SECOND FLOOR: 973 SQ. FT.
- TOTAL: 3,167 SQ. FT.
- BONUS SPACE: 281 SQ. FT.
- BEDROOMS: 4
- BATHROOMS: 3½
- WIDTH: 71'-11"
- DEPTH: 54'-4"

SEARCH ONLINE @ EPLANS.COM

This updated farmhouse has been given additional custom-styled features. Twin gables, sidelights, and an arched entryway accent the facade, while decorative ceiling treatments, bay windows, and French doors adorn the interior. From an abundance of counter space and large walk-in pantry to the built-ins and storage areas, this design makes the most of space. Supported by columns, a curved balcony overlooks the stunning two-story great room. The powder room is easily accessible from the common rooms, and angled corners soften the dining room.

SECOND FLOOR

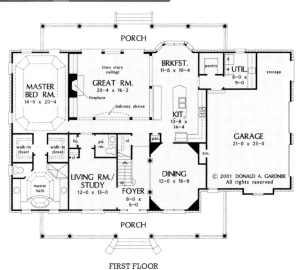

FIRST FLOOR

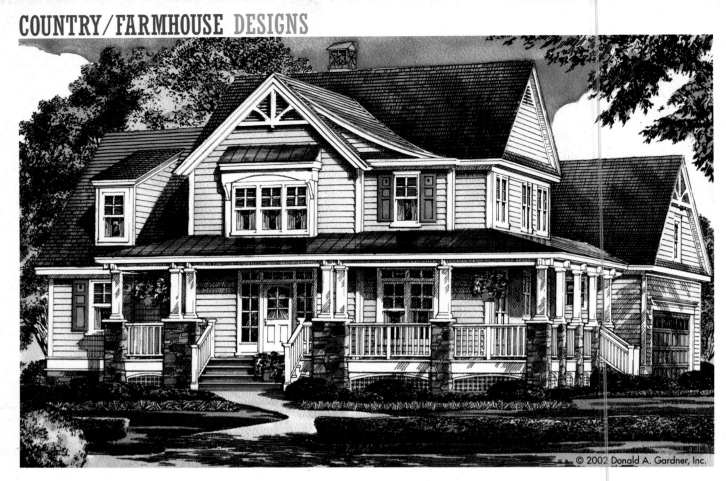

An expansive wraparound porch creates a comfortable country feel for this design; inside, an open floor plan adds a carefree attitude. A soaring two-story ceiling enhances the great room, which is open to the kitchen and breakfast area. A cozy rear porch is accessible from the great room and master suite; additional master-suite features include a tray ceiling, walk-in closet and private bath. Three family bedrooms share a full bath on the second floor.

plan # HPT910050

- **STYLE: COUNTRY**
- **FIRST FLOOR: 1,687 SQ. FT.**
- **SECOND FLOOR: 807 SQ. FT.**
- **TOTAL: 2,494 SQ. FT.**
- **BEDROOMS: 4**
- **BATHROOMS: 2½**
- **WIDTH: 52'-8"**
- **DEPTH: 67'-0"**

SEARCH ONLINE @ EPLANS.COM

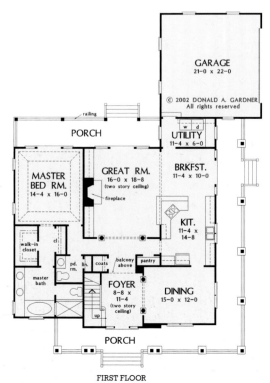

FIRST FLOOR

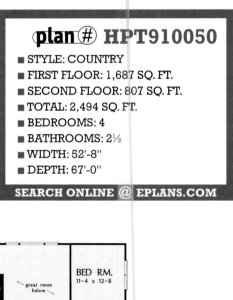

SECOND FLOOR

TO ORDER BLUEPRINTS CALL TOLL FREE 1-800-521-6797

Plan HPT910052; see page 98 for details.

CRAFTSMAN/BUNGALOW DESIGNS

Exquisite details and distinctive styling make these
designs works of art that you'll be proud to call home.

Cathedral ceilings bring a feeling of spaciousness to this home. The great room features a fireplace, cathedral ceilings and built-in bookshelves. The kitchen is designed for efficient use with its food preparation island and pantry. The master suite provides a welcome retreat with a cathedral ceiling, a walk-in closet and a luxurious bath. Two additional bedrooms, one with a walk-in closet, share a skylit bath. A second-floor bonus room is perfect for a study or a play area.

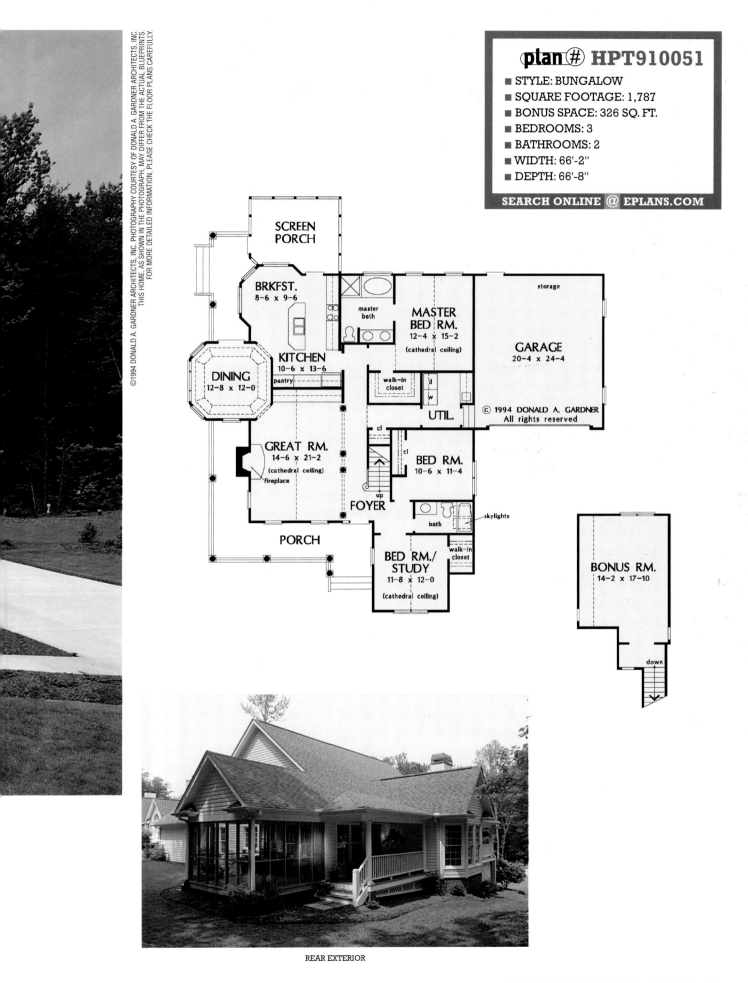

plan# HPT910051

- STYLE: BUNGALOW
- SQUARE FOOTAGE: 1,787
- BONUS SPACE: 326 SQ. FT.
- BEDROOMS: 3
- BATHROOMS: 2
- WIDTH: 66'-2"
- DEPTH: 66'-8"

SEARCH ONLINE @ EPLANS.COM

SCREEN PORCH

BRKFST.
8-6 x 9-6

master bath

MASTER BED RM.
12-4 x 15-2
(cathedral ceiling)

storage

GARAGE
20-4 x 24-4

KITCHEN
10-6 x 13-6

pantry

DINING
12-8 x 12-0

walk-in closet

d w

UTIL.

GREAT RM.
14-6 x 21-2
(cathedral ceiling)
fireplace

cl

cl

BED RM.
10-6 x 11-4

up

FOYER

bath

skylights

PORCH

walk-in closet

BED RM./ STUDY
11-8 x 12-0
(cathedral ceiling)

BONUS RM.
14-2 x 17-10

down

REAR EXTERIOR

Looking a bit like a mountain resort, this fine Craftsman home is sure to be the envy of your neighborhood. Entering through the elegant front door, one finds an open staircase to the right and a spacious great room directly ahead. Here, a fireplace and a wall of windows give a cozy welcome. A lavish master suite begins with a sitting room, complete with a fireplace, and continues to a private porch, large walk-in closet and sumptuous bedroom area. The gourmet kitchen adjoins a sunny dining room and offers access to a screened porch.

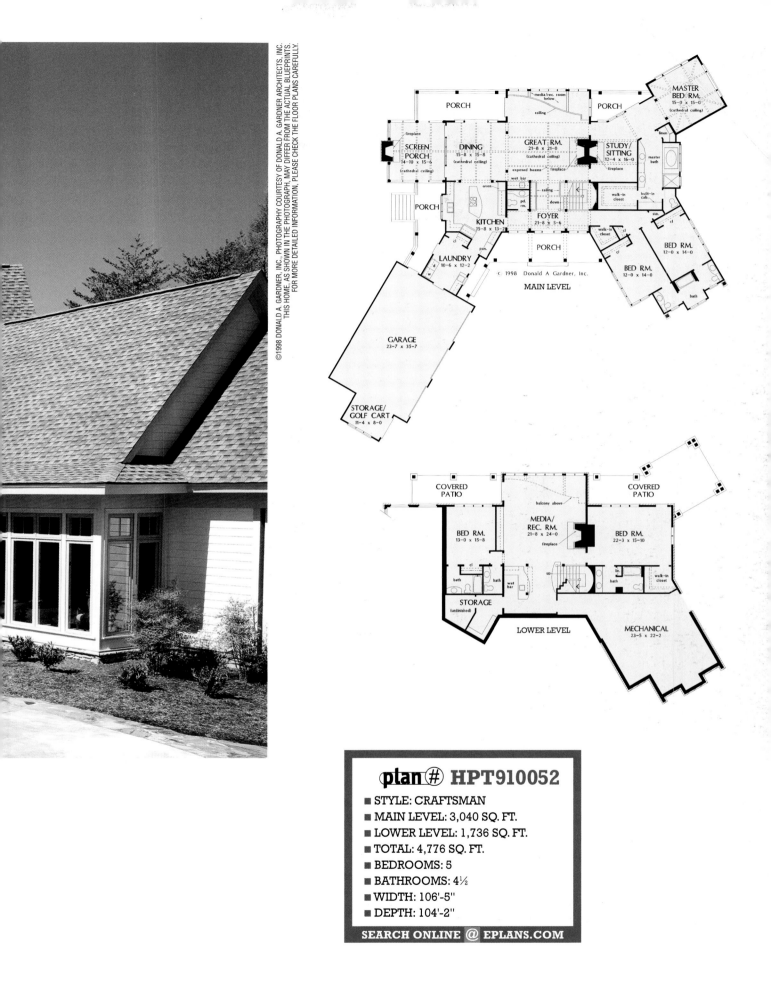

MAIN LEVEL

LOWER LEVEL

ptan# HPT910052

- STYLE: CRAFTSMAN
- MAIN LEVEL: 3,040 SQ. FT.
- LOWER LEVEL: 1,736 SQ. FT.
- TOTAL: 4,776 SQ. FT.
- BEDROOMS: 5
- BATHROOMS: 4½
- WIDTH: 106'-5"
- DEPTH: 104'-2"

SEARCH ONLINE @ EPLANS.COM

CRAFTSMAN/BUNGALOW DESIGNS

A prominent center gable with an arched window accents the facade of this custom Craftsman home, which features an exterior of cedar shakes, siding and stone. An open floor plan with generously proportioned rooms contributes to the home's spacious and relaxed atmosphere. The vaulted great room boasts a rear wall of windows, a fireplace bordered by built-in cabinets, and convenient access to the kitchen. A second-floor loft overlooks the great room for added drama. The master suite is completely secluded and enjoys a cathedral ceiling, back-porch access, a large walk-in closet and a luxurious bath. The home includes three additional bedrooms and baths as well as a vaulted loft/study and a bonus room.

plan# HPT910053

- **STYLE: CRAFTSMAN**
- **FIRST FLOOR: 2,477 SQ. FT.**
- **SECOND FLOOR: 742 SQ. FT.**
- **TOTAL: 3,219 SQ. FT.**
- **BONUS SPACE: 419 SQ. FT.**
- **BEDROOMS: 4**
- **BATHROOMS: 4**
- **WIDTH: 100'-0"**
- **DEPTH: 66'-2"**

SEARCH ONLINE @ EPLANS.COM

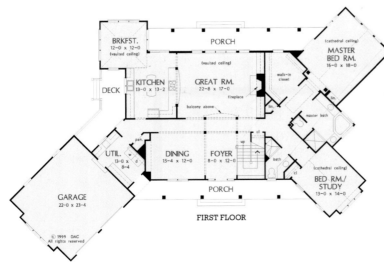

FIRST FLOOR

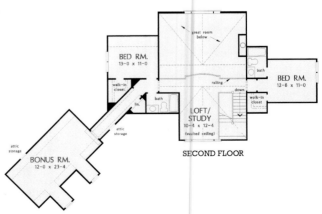

SECOND FLOOR

TO ORDER BLUEPRINTS CALL TOLL FREE 1-800-521-6797

© 1999 Donald A. Gardner, Inc.

plan # HPT910054

- **STYLE: CRAFTSMAN**
- **MAIN LEVEL: 1,662 SQ. FT.**
- **UPPER LEVEL: 585 SQ. FT.**
- **LOWER LEVEL: 706 SQ. FT.**
- **TOTAL: 2,953 SQ. FT.**
- **BONUS SPACE: 575 SQ. FT.**
- **BEDROOMS: 4**
- **BATHROOMS: 3½**
- **WIDTH: 81'-4"**
- **DEPTH: 68'-8"**

SEARCH ONLINE @ EPLANS.COM

A stunning center dormer with an arched window embellishes the exterior of this Craftsman-style home. The dormer's arched window allows light into the foyer and built-in niche. The second-floor hall is a balcony that overlooks both the foyer and great room. A generous back porch extends the great room, which features an impressive vaulted ceiling and fireplace, while a tray ceiling adorns the formal dining room. The master suite, which includes a tray ceiling as well, enjoys back-porch access, a built-in cabinet, generous walk-in closet and private bath. Two more bedrooms are located upstairs, while a fourth can be found in the basement along with a family room.

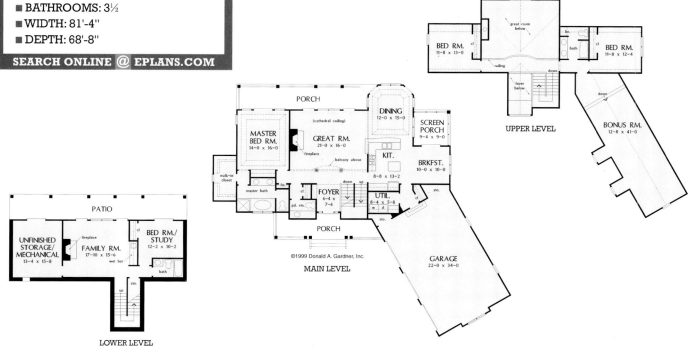

©1999 Donald A. Gardner, Inc.

MAIN LEVEL

UPPER LEVEL

LOWER LEVEL

© 2001 Donald A. Gardner, Inc.

This incredible home evokes images of stately ranches with classic wood detailing and deep eaves. An arched entryway mimics the large clerestory above it, while a trio of dormers and multiple gables add architectural interest. Equally impressive, the interior boasts three fireplaces — one within a scenic screened porch — while a long cathedral ceiling extends from the great room to the screened porch and is highlighted by exposed beams. An art niche complements the foyer, and a wet bar enhances the great room. Columns help distinguish rooms without enclosing space. The extraordinary master suite features a large study/sitting area, bedroom with exposed beams in a hipped cathedral ceiling, huge walk-in closet and spacious master bath.

plan# HPT910055

- **STYLE: CRAFTSMAN**
- **SQUARE FOOTAGE: 3,188**
- **BONUS SPACE: 615 SQ. FT.**
- **BEDROOMS: 3**
- **BATHROOMS: 2½**
- **WIDTH: 106'-4"**
- **DEPTH: 104'-1"**

SEARCH ONLINE @ EPLANS.COM

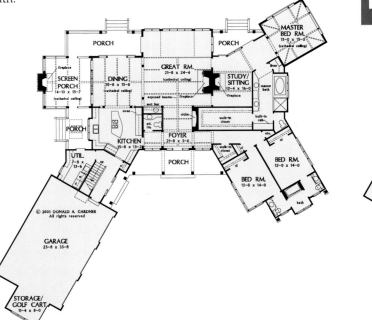

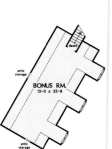

TO ORDER BLUEPRINTS CALL TOLL FREE 1-800-521-6797

© 2000 Donald A. Gardner, Inc.

plan # HPT910056

- STYLE: CRAFTSMAN
- FIRST FLOOR: 2,477 SQ. FT.
- SECOND FLOOR: 742 SQ. FT.
- TOTAL: 3,219 SQ. FT.
- BONUS SPACE: 419 SQ. FT.
- BEDROOMS: 4
- BATHROOMS: 4
- WIDTH: 99'-10"
- DEPTH: 66'-2"

SEARCH ONLINE @ EPLANS.COM

This elegant design brings back the sophistication and elegance of days gone by, yet its modern layout creates a natural traffic flow to enhance easy living. Columns partition space without enclosing it, while built-ins in the great room and counter space in the utility/mud room add convenience. The family-friendly floor plan can be witnessed in the kitchen's handy pass-through, and the kitchen has access to the rear porch for outdoor entertaining. Cathedral ceilings highlight the master bedroom and bedroom/study, while vaulted ceilings top the breakfast area and loft/study. The bonus room can be used as a home theater, playroom, or gym, and its position allows it to keep recreational noise away from the house proper.

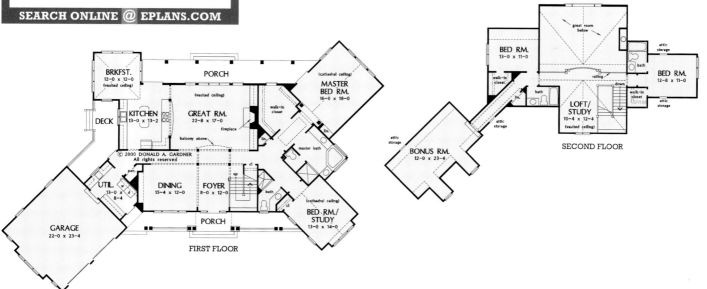

Stone accents, dormer windows and a petite front porch highlight the exterior of this Craftsman design. Inside, unique ceiling treatments make this design stand out—the great room, dining room and kitchen all boast cathedral ceilings, while the master bedroom offers a soaring vaulted ceiling. Other enticing features include a covered rear porch—accessible from the great room, dining room, breakfast nook and master suite—two walk-in closets in the master suite, and a spacious bonus room above the garage.

plan# HPT910057

- STYLE: CRAFTSMAN
- SQUARE FOOTAGE: 1,911
- BONUS SPACE: 366 SQ. FT.
- BEDROOMS: 3
- BATHROOMS: 2
- WIDTH: 52'-0"
- DEPTH: 69'-10"

SEARCH ONLINE @ EPLANS.COM

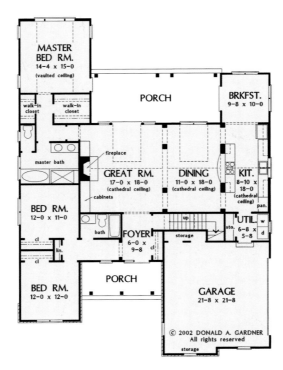

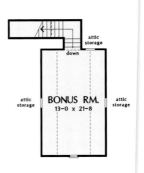

© 2000 Donald A. Gardner, Inc.

plan# HPT910058

- **STYLE: CRAFTSMAN**
- **MAIN LEVEL: 1,682 SQ. FT.**
- **UPPER LEVEL: 577 SQ. FT.**
- **LOWER LEVEL: 690 SQ. FT.**
- **TOTAL: 2,949 SQ. FT.**
- **BONUS SPACE: 459 SQ. FT.**
- **BEDROOMS: 4**
- **BATHROOMS: 3½**
- **WIDTH: 79'-0"**
- **DEPTH: 68'-2"**

SEARCH ONLINE @ EPLANS.COM

Stone and siding combine to give this Craftsman design striking curb appeal. A portico sets the tone with a gentle arch and four stately columns. A clerestory above the front entrance floods the two-story foyer with natural light. Inside, Old World charm gives way to an open, family-efficient floor plan. The kitchen partitions the dining room and breakfast area and easily accesses a screen porch for outdoor entertaining. The great room features a two-story fireplace and French doors that lead to the rear porch. A family room also sports a fireplace and patio access. The master bedroom is crowned by a tray ceiling, while a balcony with a curved alcove separates two additional bedrooms upstairs.

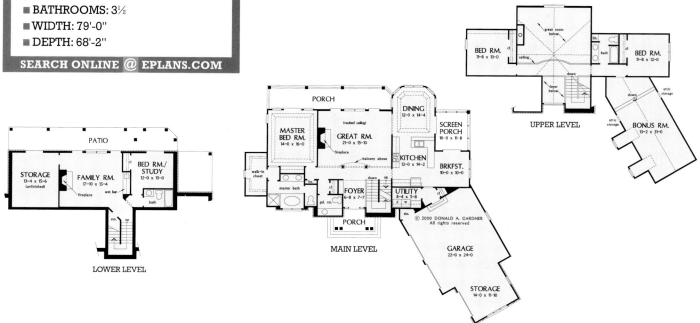

Graceful arches contrast with high gables for a stunning exterior on this Craftsman home. Windows with decorative transoms and several French doors flood the open floor plan with natural light. Tray ceilings in the dining room and master bedroom as well as cathedral ceilings in the bedroom/study, great room, kitchen and breakfast area create architectural interest and visual space. Built-ins in the great room and additional space in the garage offer convenient storage. A screened porch allows for comfortable outdoor entertaining; a bonus room, near two additional bedrooms, offers flexibility. Positioned for privacy, the master suite features access to the screened porch, dual walk-in closets and a well-appointed bath, including a private toilet, garden tub, double vanity and spacious shower.

plan# HPT910059

- **STYLE: CRAFTSMAN**
- **SQUARE FOOTAGE: 2,097**
- **BONUS SPACE: 352 SQ. FT.**
- **BEDROOMS: 4**
- **BATHROOMS: 3**
- **WIDTH: 64'-10"**
- **DEPTH: 59'-6"**

SEARCH ONLINE @ EPLANS.COM

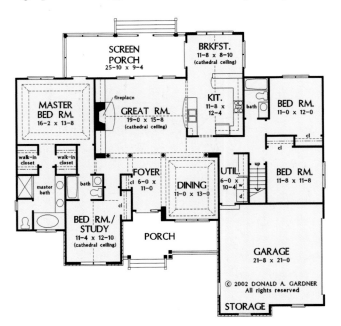

TO ORDER BLUEPRINTS CALL TOLL FREE 1-800-521-6797

© 2002 Donald A. Gardner, Inc.

plan# HPT910060

- STYLE: CRAFTSMAN
- SQUARE FOOTAGE: 1,580
- BONUS SPACE: 367 SQ. FT.
- BEDROOMS: 3
- BATHROOMS: 2
- WIDTH: 55'-6"
- DEPTH: 46'-0"

SEARCH ONLINE @ EPLANS.COM

A box-bay window with a standing-seam canopy decorates the front of this stone and siding Craftsman home. A vaulted ceiling accents the bedroom/study, and a cathedral ceiling enhances the central great room, which opens to a rear deck. The efficient kitchen boasts plenty of counter space and adjoins the dining room, which offers a tray ceiling and plenty of windows. The master bedroom, also with a tray ceiling, includes a walk-in closet and a private bath with a separate tub and shower and a compartmented toilet.

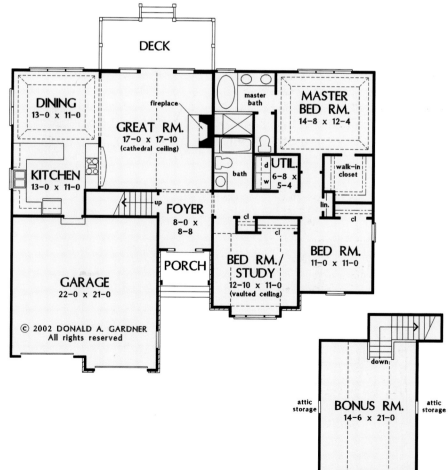

DECK

DINING
13-0 x 11-0

GREAT RM.
17-0 x 17-10
(cathedral ceiling)

fireplace

master bath

MASTER BED RM.
14-8 x 12-4

KITCHEN
13-0 x 11-0

bath

UTIL.
6-8 x 5-4

walk-in closet

up

FOYER
8-0 x 8-8

lin.

cl

cl

GARAGE
22-0 x 21-0

PORCH

BED RM./STUDY
12-10 x 11-0
(vaulted ceiling)

BED RM.
11-0 x 11-0

down

attic storage

BONUS RM.
14-6 x 21-0

attic storage

© 2001 Donald A. Gardner, Inc.

Stone and horizontal siding give a definite country flavor to this two-story home. The front study makes an ideal guest room with the adjoining powder room. The formal dining room is accented with decorative columns that define its perimeter. The great room boasts a fireplace, built-ins and a magnificent view of the backyard beyond one of two rear porches. The master suite boasts two walk-in closets and a private bath. Two bedrooms share a full bath on the second floor.

plan# HPT910061

- **STYLE: CRAFTSMAN**
- **FIRST FLOOR: 1,707 SQ. FT.**
- **SECOND FLOOR: 514 SQ. FT.**
- **TOTAL: 2,221 SQ. FT.**
- **BONUS SPACE: 211 SQ. FT.**
- **BEDROOMS: 4**
- **BATHROOMS: 2½**
- **WIDTH: 50'-0"**
- **DEPTH: 71'-8"**

SEARCH ONLINE @ EPLANS.COM

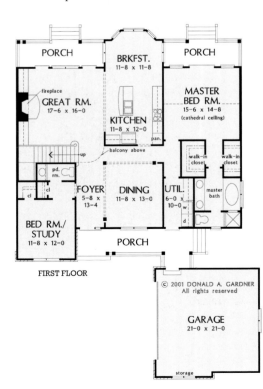

© 2001 Donald A. Gardner, Inc.

plan# HPT910062

- STYLE: CRAFTSMAN
- FIRST FLOOR: 1,547 SQ. FT.
- SECOND FLOOR: 684 SQ. FT.
- TOTAL: 2,231 SQ. FT.
- BONUS SPACE: 300 SQ. FT.
- BEDROOMS: 3
- BATHROOMS: 2½
- WIDTH: 59'-2"
- DEPTH: 44'-4"

SEARCH ONLINE @ EPLANS.COM

Stone and siding create this home's stunning exterior, along with a sloped roofline and a decorative wood bracket. A metal roof embellishes the garage's box-bay window, and arches are echoed throughout. The great room is filled with light from its many windows and French doors, and a glimpse of the warming fireplace can be seen from every gathering room. The master bedroom is graced with a cathedral ceiling and large walk-in closet. The family loft makes a perfect sitting or study area that receives a lot of light from the open, two-story great room. The second floor bathroom includes twin vanities, and the versatile bonus room is easily accessible.

FIRST FLOOR

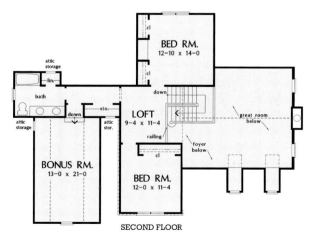

SECOND FLOOR

(vaulted ceiling)

MASTER BED RM.
13-0 x 16-0

walk-in closet

walk-in closet

BRKFST.
9-0 x 9-0

PORCH
skylights

BED RM.
11-0 x 13-0

cl

bath

UTILITY
10-8 x 6-0

KIT.
11-4 x 14-4

GREAT RM.
19-4 x 16-0

fireplace

lin.

d   w

FOYER
5-8 x 8-8

cl

GARAGE
22-4 x 21-2

DINING
11-0 x 13-0

BED RM.
11-0 x 13-0

PORCH

storage

plan# HPT910063

- STYLE: BUNGALOW
- SQUARE FOOTAGE: 1,966
- BEDROOMS: 3
- BATHROOMS: 2
- WIDTH: 54'-11"
- DEPTH: 65'-9"

SEARCH ONLINE @ EPLANS.COM

Old World charm mingles and merges with traditional detailing upon the facade of this three-bedroom home. The covered entry opens to the foyer where open planning allows views through the stately great room and out beyond the skylit rear porch. The formal dining room enjoys a tray ceiling, the master bedroom has a vaulted ceiling and the great room boasts a stepped-ceiling treatment. The angled kitchen adjoins the sunny breakfast nook while being out of sight, but not out of reach, of the dining room. On the right, the full bath lends privacy to the two family bedrooms.

plan# HPT910064

- STYLE: CRAFTSMAN
- SQUARE FOOTAGE: 1,904
- BONUS SPACE: 366 SQ. FT.
- BEDROOMS: 3
- BATHROOMS: 2
- WIDTH: 53'-10"
- DEPTH: 57'-8"

SEARCH ONLINE @ EPLANS.COM

Blending stone with siding, this cottage has many wonderful architectural features: an arch and column porch, metal roof on a box bay window, decorative vents and striking shed dormer. Built-in cabinetry in the great room, tray ceilings in the dining room and master bedroom and a cooktop island are just a few of the lush amenities. A pass-through connects the great room and kitchen—visually and conveniently. The master suite includes dual walk-in closets, a double vanity, private toilet, garden tub and separate shower. The study/bedroom and bonus room allow for versatility and expansion to meet the family's changing needs.

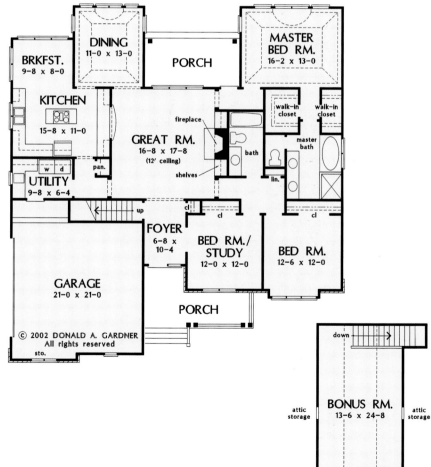

© 2001 Donald A. Gardner, Inc.

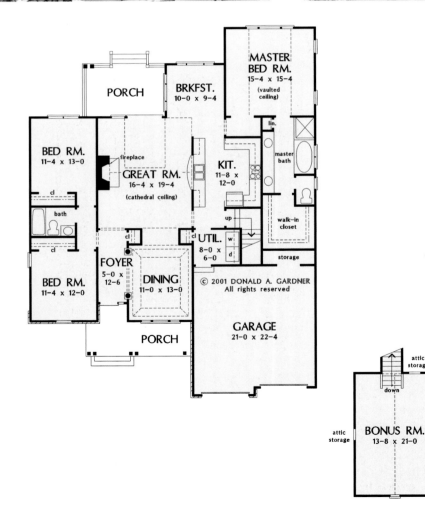

plan# HPT910065

- STYLE: CRAFTSMAN
- SQUARE FOOTAGE: 1,857
- BONUS SPACE: 352 SQ. FT.
- BEDROOMS: 3
- BATHROOMS: 2
- WIDTH: 50'-0"
- DEPTH: 64'-8"

SEARCH ONLINE @ EPLANS.COM

A mixture of stone and siding embraces an ageless style. Gables are enhanced by ornamental wood brackets and vents, while twin dormers add symmetrical balance to the front elevation. Decorative ceiling treatments—from cathedral to tray—can be found throughout this floor plan. Columns, a pass-through and a low wall are used to distinguish rooms and keep areas open. The dining room features an arch that leads to the great room, which is accented by a fireplace and French doors that access the porch. The garage features a spacious storage closet and a bonus room above. Note the convenient location of the utility room.

© 2001 Donald A. Gardner, Inc.

plan# HPT910066

- STYLE: CRAFTSMAN
- SQUARE FOOTAGE: 1,682
- BONUS SPACE: 320 SQ. FT.
- BEDROOMS: 3
- BATHROOMS: 2
- WIDTH: 40'-0"
- DEPTH: 78'-4"

SEARCH ONLINE @ EPLANS.COM

This Arts and Crafts cottage combines stone and stucco to create an Old World feel. From decorative wood brackets and columns to arched windows and shutters, the details produce architectural interest and absolute charm. This design features plenty of windows and French doors to invite nature inside. Built-in cabinetry enhances the interior and provides convenience. Topping the great room is a cathedral ceiling, and a tray ceiling completes the dining room. The master suite, which features a vaulted ceiling in the bedroom and an ample master bath, lies next to the screened porch, while a bonus room, accessible from two additional bedrooms, would make a perfect game room for the family.

©2001 Donald A. Gardner, Inc.

plan# HPT910067

- **STYLE:** CRAFTSMAN
- **SQUARE FOOTAGE:** 1,753
- **BONUS SPACE:** 389 SQ. FT.
- **BEDROOMS:** 3
- **BATHROOMS:** 2
- **WIDTH:** 49'-4"
- **DEPTH:** 64'-4"

SEARCH ONLINE @ EPLANS.COM

The combination of stone and siding creates an appealing facade to complement any neighborhood. Inside, the dining room is defined by columns and features a tray ceiling. A fireplace warms up the great room and provides access to the rear deck. In the kitchen, the cooktop island and extended counter space make meal preparation simple and organized. Two family bedrooms—one that can be used as a study—share a full hall bath. The master bedroom provides a private bath with double-bowl sinks, His and Hers closets, a tub and separate shower. The utility room is located near the garage entrance.

© 2001 Donald A. Gardner, Inc.

plan # HPT910068

- STYLE: CRAFTSMAN
- SQUARE FOOTAGE: 2,252
- BEDROOMS: 3
- BATHROOMS: 2
- WIDTH: 57'-8"
- DEPTH: 64'-4"

SEARCH ONLINE @ EPLANS.COM

Though the stone and siding exterior suggest a rustic nature, the interior offers many refined elements, not the least of which is the lavish master suite. The dining room is accented with a tray ceiling and decorative columns. The great room has a vaulted ceiling, a fireplace, built-ins and a wall of windows. The island kitchen adjoins the breakfast bay. The front-facing bedroom shares a full bath with the bedroom/study. The master suite includes a bedroom with a tray ceiling, two walk-in closets and a dual-sink vanity.

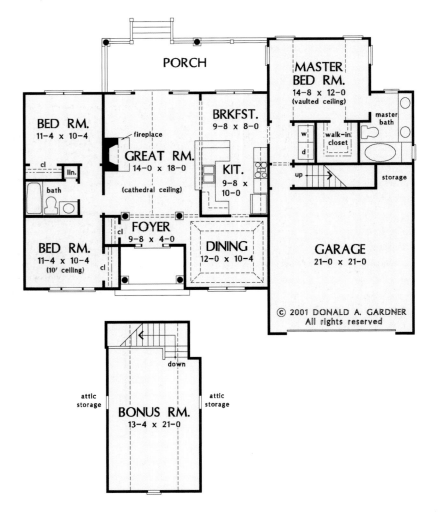

PORCH

BED RM.
11-4 x 10-4

fireplace

GREAT RM.
14-0 x 18-0
(cathedral ceiling)

BRKFST.
9-8 x 8-0

KIT.
9-8 x 10-0

MASTER BED RM.
14-8 x 12-0
(vaulted ceiling)

master bath

walk-in closet

w d

up

storage

cl

bath

lin.

FOYER
9-8 x 4-0

cl

DINING
12-0 x 10-4

GARAGE
21-0 x 21-0

BED RM.
11-4 x 10-4
(10' ceiling)

cl

attic storage

down

attic storage

BONUS RM.
13-4 x 21-0

plan⊕ HPT910069

- ■ STYLE: BUNGALOW
- ■ SQUARE FOOTAGE: 1,377
- ■ BONUS SPACE: 322 SQ. FT.
- ■ BEDROOMS: 3
- ■ BATHROOMS: 2
- ■ WIDTH: 57'-8"
- ■ DEPTH: 44'-0"

SEARCH ONLINE @ EPLANS.COM

This delightful summer cottage offers a simple layout, favorable to any family. The foyer is flanked by an elegant dining room boasting a tray ceiling and two family bedrooms that share a hall bath. The great room is enhanced by a cathedral ceiling and a warming fireplace. The gourmet kitchen is conveniently located and ready to serve the breakfast area, which showcases great views of the rear porch. The master suite boasts elegance with its vaulted ceiling, large walk-in closet and pampering private bath. Just around the corner from the master retreat is a conveniently located laundry room.

plan # HPT910070

- STYLE: BUNGALOW
- SQUARE FOOTAGE: 1,517
- BONUS SPACE: 287 SQ. FT.
- BEDROOMS: 3
- BATHROOMS: 2
- WIDTH: 61'-4"
- DEPTH: 48'-6"

SEARCH ONLINE @ EPLANS.COM

The foyer opens to a spacious great room with a fireplace and a cathedral ceiling in this lovely traditional home. Sliding doors open to a rear deck from the great room, posing a warm welcome to enjoy the outdoors. The U-shaped kitchen features an angled peninsula counter with a cooktop. A private hall leads to the family sleeping quarters, which includes two bedrooms and a full bath with a double-bowl lavatory. Sizable bonus space above the garage provides a skylight.

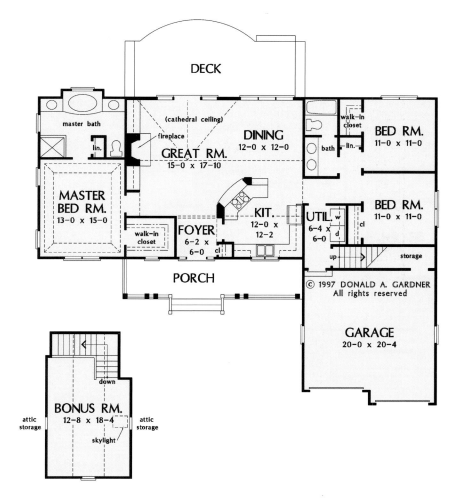

plan# HPT910071

- STYLE: CRAFTSMAN
- SQUARE FOOTAGE: 1,858
- BONUS SPACE: 365 SQ. FT.
- BEDROOMS: 3
- BATHROOMS: 2
- WIDTH: 55'-8"
- DEPTH: 64'-10"

SEARCH ONLINE @ EPLANS.COM

A smart combination of stone and siding, multiple gables and eye-catching windows contributes to the warm Craftsman style of this three-bedroom home. A tray ceiling and interior columns highlight the formal dining room, while the great room and kitchen enjoy a soaring cathedral ceiling. Built-in bookshelves border the fireplace in the great room, where a clerestory dormer brings in an abundance of natural light. A split-bedroom design places two family bedrooms and a bath with a linen closet on one side of the home and the master suite with a walk-in closet and private bath on the other.

plan # HPT910072

- STYLE: BUNGALOW
- SQUARE FOOTAGE: 1,264
- BONUS SPACE: 397 SQ. FT.
- BEDROOMS: 3
- BATHROOMS: 2
- WIDTH: 47'-0"
- DEPTH: 40'-4"

SEARCH ONLINE @ EPLANS.COM

Two dormers balanced with a double gable and arch-top windows impart poise and charm to this efficient three-bedroom home. Relax on the front porch, or go inside to warm up by the fireplace in the great room. A cathedral ceiling and windows on two walls lend a bright and fresh feel to the great room. The dining room views the front yard through a beautiful arch-top picture window. The master suite enjoys a view of the backyard, a private bath and a walk-in closet. This plan also allows for expansion into the second-floor bonus room.

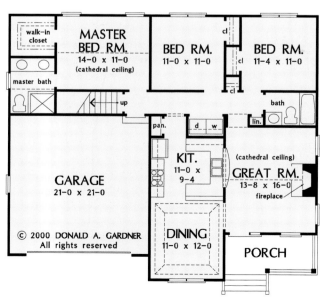

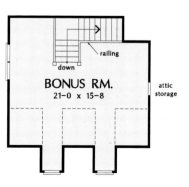

This hillside home combines stucco, stone and cedar shakes for exceptional Craftsman character. A dramatic cathedral ceiling heightens the open living room with a central fireplace and built-ins. Porches flank the living room to allow its rear wall of windows uninterrupted views of the outdoors. Exit to the two rear porches from the dining room and master bedroom, while the breakfast and dining rooms enjoy screened-porch access. A tray ceiling tops the master bedroom, which features a lovely private bath and walk-in closet. A versatile bedroom/study and full bath are nearby. Downstairs are two more bedrooms, each with an adjacent covered patio, another full bath and a generous family room with a fireplace.

plan # HPT910073

- STYLE: CRAFTSMAN
- MAIN LEVEL: 1,180 SQ. FT.
- LOWER LEVEL: 1,146 SQ. FT.
- TOTAL: 2,956 SQ. FT.
- BEDROOMS: 4
- BATHROOMS: 3
- WIDTH: 68'-4"
- DEPTH: 60'-10"

SEARCH ONLINE @ EPLANS.COM

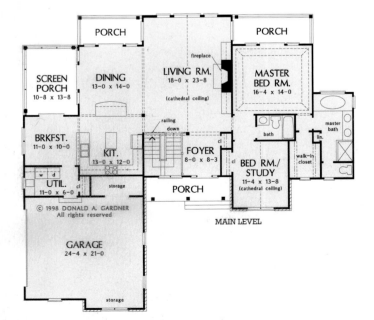

MAIN LEVEL

LOWER LEVEL

Plan HPT910075; see page 124 for details.

TRADITIONAL DESIGNS

Soaring gables and large, arched windows distinguish these homes, which feature classic style and the latest amenities.

With a decidedly European flavor, this two-story traditional home offers great livability. Classic stone and stucco formality enhances the exterior appearance. The foyer opens to a study or living room on the left — warmed by an enchanting fireplace. The dining room on the right offers large proportions and full illuminating windows. The family room with fireplace remains open to the island kitchen and breakfast room. Here, a sunny bay window overlooks the rear yard and patio. The rear patio is an entertaining dream — complete with a cozy spa. In the master suite, a bayed sitting area, walk-in closet and a pampering bath with a whirlpool tub make a fine retreat. Upstairs, two bedrooms flank a loft or study area. These family bedrooms share a full hall bath. The bonus room — brightened by beautiful skylights — easily converts to a guest bedroom, home office or playroom.

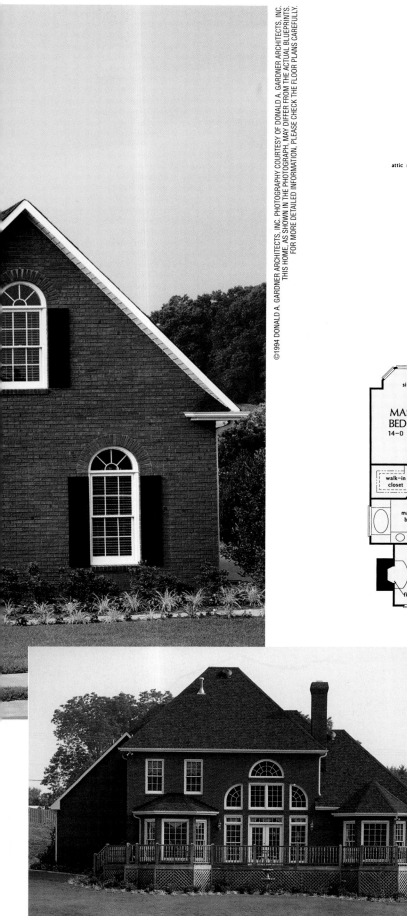

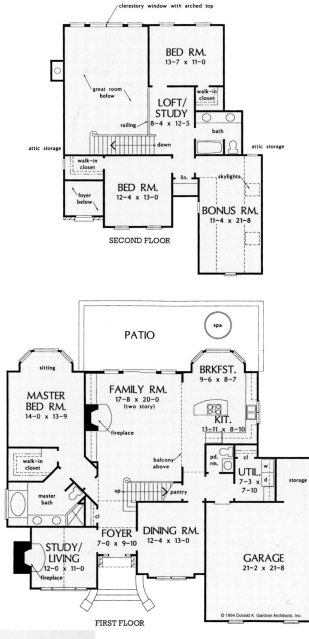

SECOND FLOOR

clerestory window with arched top

BED RM.
13-7 x 11-0

great room below

LOFT/
STUDY
8-4 x 12-5

walk-in closet

railing

bath

attic storage

down

attic storage

walk-in closet

lin.

skylights

foyer below

BED RM.
12-4 x 13-0

BONUS RM.
11-4 x 21-8

FIRST FLOOR

PATIO

spa

sitting

FAMILY RM.
17-8 x 20-0
(two story)

BRKFST.
9-6 x 8-7

MASTER
BED RM.
14-0 x 13-9

fireplace

KIT.
13-11 x 8-10

walk-in closet

balcony above

pd. rm.

cl

UTIL.
7-3 x
7-10

w
d

storage

master bath

up

pantry

cl

FOYER
7-0 x 9-10

DINING RM.
12-4 x 13-0

GARAGE
21-2 x 21-8

STUDY/
LIVING
12-0 x 11-0

fireplace

© 1994 Donald A. Gardner Architects, Inc.

REAR EXTERIOR

plan# HPT910074

- STYLE: TRADITIONAL
- FIRST FLOOR: 1,715 SQ. FT.
- SECOND FLOOR: 620 SQ. FT.
- TOTAL: 2,335 SQ. FT.
- BONUS SPACE: 265 SQ. FT.
- BEDROOMS: 3
- BATHROOMS: 2½
- WIDTH: 58'-6"
- DEPTH: 50'-3"

SEARCH ONLINE @ EPLANS.COM

SECOND FLOOR

great room below

railing

attic storage

LOFT
12-0 x 10-2

down

railing

foyer below

down

BED RM.
12-0 x 11-8

cl

lin.

down

bath

cl

attic storage

BED RM.
12-0 x 12-3

attic storage

down

attic storage

skylights

BONUS RM.
12-0 x 27-8

PATIO

(cathedral ceiling)

FAMILY RM.
18-2 x 20-10

fireplace

balcony above

BRKFST.
12-0 x 9-4

up

UTIL.
8-8 x 8-0

storage

MASTER
BED RM.
14-0 x 16-0

walk-in closet

d

cl

sto.

w

KIT.
12-0 x 13-0

walk-in closet

lin.

master bath

pd. rm.

pan.

cl

LIVING RM./
STUDY
12-0 x 13-4

FOYER
11-0 x 8-4

up

DINING
12-0 x 14-4

GARAGE
21-0 x 24-0

PORCH

© 1996 Donald A. Gardner Architects, Inc.

FIRST FLOOR

©1996 DONALD A. GARDNER ARCHITECTS, INC. PHOTOGRAPHY COURTESY OF DONALD A. GARDNER ARCHITECTS, INC. THIS HOME, AS SHOWN IN THE PHOTOGRAPH, MAY DIFFER FROM THE ACTUAL BLUEPRINTS. FOR MORE DETAILED INFORMATION, PLEASE CHECK THE FLOOR PLANS CAREFULLY.

plan # HPT910075

- STYLE: TRADITIONAL
- FIRST FLOOR: 1,904 SQ. FT.
- SECOND FLOOR: 645 SQ. FT.
- TOTAL: 2,549 SQ. FT.
- BONUS SPACE: 434 SQ. FT.
- BEDROOMS: 3
- BATHROOMS: 2½
- WIDTH: 71'-2"
- DEPTH: 45'-8"

SEARCH ONLINE @ EPLANS.COM

This stucco home contrasts gently curved arches with gables and uses large multi-pane windows to flood the interior with natural light. Square pillars form an impressive entry, leading to a two-story foyer. The living room is set apart from the informal area of the house and could serve as a cozy study instead. The back patio can be reached from both the breakfast nook and the family room, which features a cathedral ceiling and a fireplace. The master suite offers two walk-in closets and a bath with twin vanities, a garden tub and separate shower.

Arched windows and triple gables provide a touch of elegance to this traditional home. A barrel-vaulted entrance supported by columns welcomes family and guests inside. On the main level, the dining room offers round columns at the entrance. The great room boasts a cathedral ceiling, a fireplace, and an arched window over the doors to the deck. The kitchen features an island cooktop and an adjoining breakfast nook for informal dining. The master suite offers twin walk-in closets and a lavish bath that includes a whirlpool tub and a double-basin vanity.

BED RM.
10-4 × 11-9

walk-in closet

down

cl

bath

BED RM.
12-4 × 13-6

BONUS RM.
11-0 × 20-0

down

SECOND FLOOR

QUOTE ONE®

Cost to build? See page 186
to order complete cost estimate
to build this house in your area!

seat

DECK

spa

arched window above door

GREAT RM.
15-4 × 18-0
(cathedral ceiling)

fireplace

KIT./BRKFST.
16-8 × 16-0

master bath

walk-in closet

walk-in closet

pd. rm.

up

sto.

UTILITY
10-0 × 6-4

w
d

MASTER BED RM.
13-0 × 13-6

cl

FOYER
7-8 × 9-0

DINING
12-4 × 12-4

up

storage

PORCH

GARAGE
20-0 × 20-0

©1991 Donald A. Gardner Architects, Inc.

FIRST FLOOR

plan# HPT910076

- **STYLE: TRADITIONAL**
- **FIRST FLOOR: 1,416 SQ. FT.**
- **SECOND FLOOR: 445 SQ. FT.**
- **TOTAL: 1,861 SQ. FT.**
- **BONUS SPACE: 284 SQ. FT.**
- **BEDROOMS: 3**
- **BATHROOMS: 2½**
- **WIDTH: 58'-3"**
- **DEPTH: 68'-6"**

SEARCH ONLINE @ EPLANS.COM

REAR EXTERIOR

TRADITIONAL DESIGNS

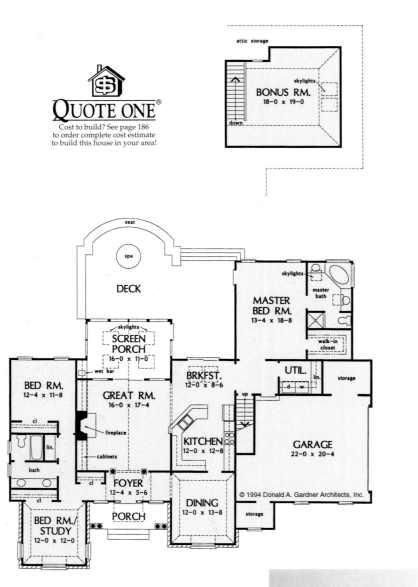

QUOTE ONE®

Cost to build? See page 186
to order complete cost estimate
to build this house in your area!

attic storage

BONUS RM.
18-0 x 19-0

skylights

down

seat
spa

DECK

SCREEN PORCH
16-0 x 11-0

skylights

wet bar

BED RM.
12-4 x 11-8

GREAT RM.
16-0 x 17-4

fireplace

cabinets

cl

bath

lin.

BRKFST.
12-0 x 8-6

KITCHEN
12-0 x 12-8

up

MASTER BED RM.
13-4 x 18-8

master bath

skylights

walk-in closet

UTIL.
d-w-

lin.

storage

GARAGE
22-0 x 20-4

FOYER
12-4 x 5-6

DINING
12-0 x 13-8

storage

BED RM./STUDY
12-0 x 12-0

PORCH

© 1994 Donald A. Gardner Architects, Inc.

plan# HPT910077

- STYLE: TRADITIONAL
- SQUARE FOOTAGE: 1,977
- BONUS SPACE: 430 SQ. FT.
- BEDROOMS: 3
- BATHROOMS: 2
- WIDTH: 69'-8"
- DEPTH: 59'-6"

SEARCH ONLINE @ EPLANS.COM

REAR EXTERIOR

A two-story foyer with a Palladian window above sets the tone for this sunlit home. Columns mark the passage from the foyer to the great room, where a central fireplace and built-in cabinets are found. A screened porch with four skylights above and a wet bar provides a pleasant place to start the day or wind down after work. The kitchen is flanked by the formal dining room and the breakfast room. Hidden quietly at the rear, the master suite includes a bath with dual vanities and skylights. Two family bedrooms (one an optional study) share a bath that has twin sinks.

This attractive three-bedroom house offers a touch of country with its covered front porch. The foyer, flanked by the dining room and the bedroom/study, leads to the spacious great room. Here, a fireplace and window wall enhance any gathering. The U-shaped kitchen features a window over the sink and a serving counter to the breakfast room. The dining room and breakfast room have cathedral ceilings with arched windows that fill the house with natural light. The master bedroom boasts a cathedral ceiling and a bath with a whirlpool tub, shower and double-bowl vanity. Two family bedrooms reside upstairs.

plan # HPT910078

- STYLE: TRADITIONAL
- FIRST FLOOR: 1,675 SQ. FT.
- SECOND FLOOR: 448 SQ. FT.
- TOTAL: 2,123 SQ. FT.
- BONUS SPACE: 345 SQ. FT.
- BEDROOMS: 4
- BATHROOMS: 3
- WIDTH: 53'-8"
- DEPTH: 69'-8"

SEARCH ONLINE @ EPLANS.COM

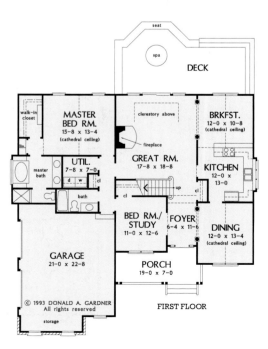

FIRST FLOOR

SECOND FLOOR

TO ORDER BLUEPRINTS CALL TOLL FREE 1-800-521-6797

© 1998 Donald A. Gardner, Inc.

plan # HPT910079

- STYLE: TRADITIONAL
- SQUARE FOOTAGE: 2,262
- BONUS SPACE: 388 SQ. FT.
- BEDROOMS: 4
- BATHROOMS: 2½
- WIDTH: 77'-4"
- DEPTH: 62'-0"

SEARCH ONLINE @ EPLANS.COM

True tradition is exhibited in the brick and siding facade, hipped roof, and keystone arches of this spacious four-bedroom home. Stately columns framing the front entry are repeated in the home's formal foyer. The generous great room is exemplary, boasting a fireplace with flanking built-ins. A dramatic cathedral ceiling enhances the space and is continued out into the adjoining screened porch. The nearby breakfast area is enriched by dual skylights. Three family bedrooms, two with walk-in closets, share an impressive hall bath with a dual sink vanity. Secluded on the opposite side of the home, the master suite features rear-deck access, a walk-in closet, and a private bath with a corner tub and separate vanities.

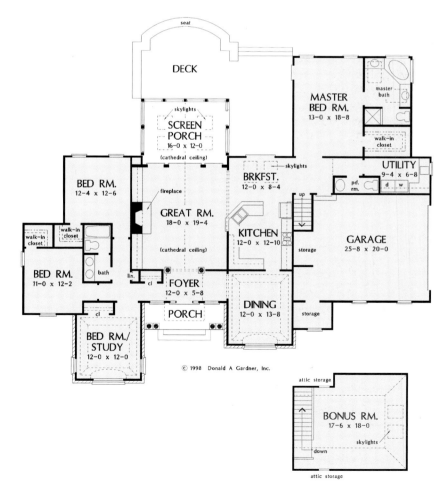

© 2002 Donald A. Gardner, Inc.

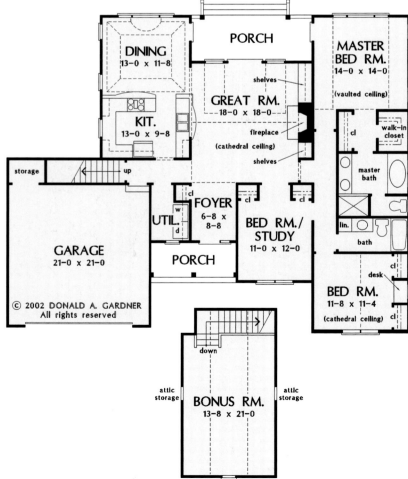

DINING
13-0 x 11-8

PORCH

MASTER BED RM.
14-0 x 14-0

(vaulted ceiling)

shelves

GREAT RM.
18-0 x 18-0

KIT.
13-0 x 9-8

fireplace

(cathedral ceiling)

shelves

walk-in closet

cl

master bath

lin.

storage

up

bath

FOYER
6-8 x 8-8

UTIL.

w
d

cl

cl

cl

BED RM./ STUDY
11-0 x 12-0

GARAGE
21-0 x 21-0

PORCH

© 2002 DONALD A. GARDNER
All rights reserved

desk

BED RM.
11-8 x 11-4

(cathedral ceiling)

cl

cl

down

attic storage

attic storage

BONUS RM.
13-8 x 21-0

plan # HPT910080

- STYLE: TRADITIONAL
- SQUARE FOOTAGE: 1,654
- BONUS SPACE: 356 SQ. FT.
- BEDROOMS: 3
- BATHROOMS: 2
- WIDTH: 60'-4"
- DEPTH: 47'-10"

SEARCH ONLINE @ EPLANS.COM

This traditional design creates wonderful indoor/outdoor relationships—a cozy front porch welcomes family and friends, and a rear porch is accessible from the great room, dining room and master suite. The dining room, placed to the rear of the plan to take advantage of rear-property views, is distinguished by a tray ceiling; the master bedroom features a vaulted ceiling. The great room and a front bedroom showcase cathedral ceilings. The efficient kitchen includes counters that spill over into the great room and dining room, providing space for elegant buffet dinners or family meals at the snack bar. A bonus room sits above the garage, ready to be converted to a recreation room, children's play area or computer center.

© 1998 Donald A. Gardner, Inc.

plan # HPT910081

- STYLE: TRADITIONAL
- SQUARE FOOTAGE: 2,024
- BONUS SPACE: 423 SQ. FT.
- BEDROOMS: 3
- BATHROOMS: 2½
- WIDTH: 62'-3"
- DEPTH: 74'-9"

SEARCH ONLINE @ EPLANS.COM

This comfortable home has more than just elegance, style and a host of amenities—it has heart. A cathedral ceiling highlights the great room, while sliding glass doors allow sunlight and access to the rear deck. Broad windows in the breakfast bay splash the angled kitchen with natural light. The private master suite boasts luxurious amenities in the master bath, such as two walk-in closets, separate lavatories and a garden tub.

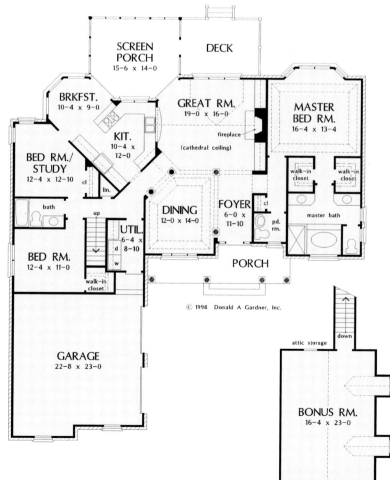

© 1998 Donald A Gardner, Inc.

© 2001 Donald A. Gardner, Inc.

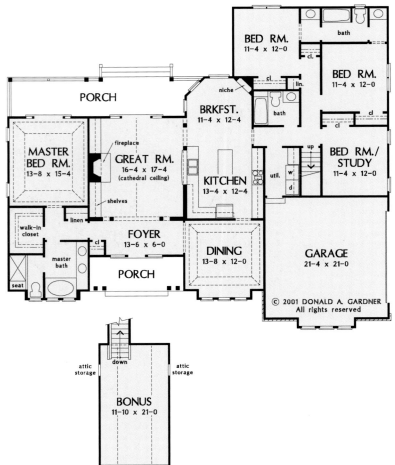

© 2001 Donald A. Gardner
All rights reserved

plan# HPT910082

- STYLE: TRADITIONAL
- SQUARE FOOTAGE: 2,174
- BONUS SPACE: 299 SQ. FT.
- BEDROOMS: 4
- BATHROOMS: 3
- WIDTH: 66'-8"
- DEPTH: 56'-6"

SEARCH ONLINE @ EPLANS.COM

This striking house combines traditional design with Craftsman materials. Twin dormers and columns establish a symmetrical frame to the entryway, and stone accents the garage's box-bay window. Built-ins, a vaulted ceiling and a fireplace highlight the great room, which is connected to the kitchen by a handy pass-through. Tray ceilings crown both the dining room and master bedroom, while French doors in the master bedroom and great room lead to the rear porch. A study/bedroom and bonus room allow for versatility, and the master suite is located for optimum privacy.

B. NATHAN

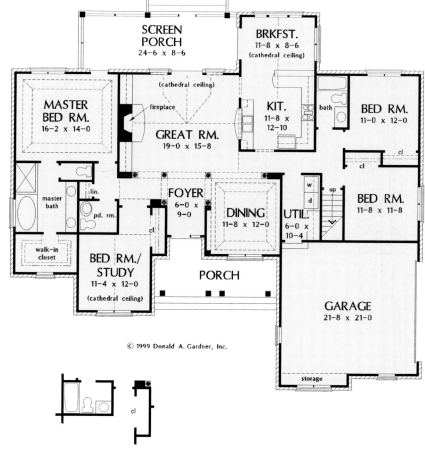

plan⊕ HPT910083

- STYLE: TRADITIONAL
- SQUARE FOOTAGE: 2,151
- BONUS SPACE: 354 SQ. FT.
- BEDROOMS: 4
- BATHROOMS: 2½
- WIDTH: 65'-9"
- DEPTH: 60'-5"

SEARCH ONLINE @ EPLANS.COM

Graceful arches complement the front porch and echo the elegant arched windows on the facade of this four-bedroom brick home. Stunning cathedral ceilings enhance the great room, kitchen, breakfast room and bedroom/study; the dining room and master bedroom enjoy distinctive tray ceilings. A fireplace flanked by built-in shelves and cabinets creates warmth and interest in the great room, which opens to a generous screened porch. Also boasting access to the porch, the master suite features a well-appointed bath and walk-in closet. The versatile bedroom/study has a single-door option for enlarging the adjacent powder room into a full bath.

SCREEN PORCH
24-6 x 8-6

BRKFST.
11-8 x 8-6
(cathedral ceiling)

(cathedral ceiling)

fireplace

KIT.
11-8 x 12-10

bath

BED RM.
11-0 x 12-0

MASTER BED RM.
16-2 x 14-0

GREAT RM.
19-0 x 15-8

cl

cl

master bath

lin.

pd. rm.

FOYER
6-0 x 9-0

DINING
11-8 x 12-0

UTIL.
6-0 x 10-4

w
d

up

BED RM.
11-8 x 11-8

walk-in closet

cl

BED RM./ STUDY
11-4 x 12-0
(cathedral ceiling)

PORCH

GARAGE
21-8 x 21-0

storage

© 1999 Donald A. Gardner, Inc.

cl

(optional full bath)

© 2000 Donald A. Gardner, Inc.

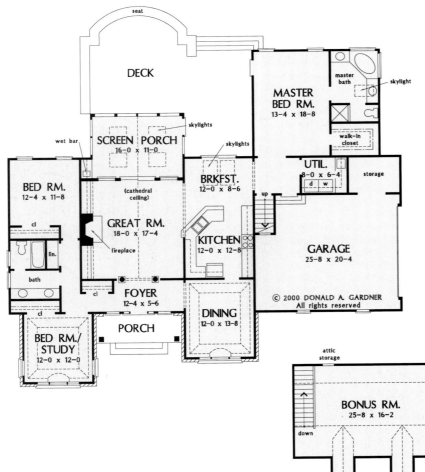

© 2000 DONALD A. GARDNER
All rights reserved

plan # HPT910084

- **STYLE:** TRADITIONAL
- **SQUARE FOOTAGE:** 1,989
- **BONUS SPACE:** 469 SQ. FT.
- **BEDROOMS:** 3
- **BATHROOMS:** 2
- **WIDTH:** 69'-8"
- **DEPTH:** 59'-6"

SEARCH ONLINE @ EPLANS.COM

Equipped with dormers, arched windows, and skylights, this executive home is flooded with light and space. Designed for elegance and versatility, the bedroom/study, screened porch with wet bar, and bonus room are elements of a home that can meet different needs for any family. The great room—with its cathedral ceiling, fireplace and built-in cabinets—is a comfortable place for everyday life as well as entertaining. Copious closet and storage space add to the smart floor plan. The large master suite has access to the deck, as well as a sizable walk-in closet. A garden tub, along with His and Hers lavatories, creates a master bath with luxury and convenience.

TO ORDER BLUEPRINTS CALL TOLL FREE 1-800-521-6797

© 2001 Donald A. Gardner, Inc.

plan# HPT910085

- STYLE: TRADITIONAL
- SQUARE FOOTAGE: 2,461
- BONUS SPACE: 397 SQ. FT.
- BEDROOMS: 4
- BATHROOMS: 2
- WIDTH: 71'-2"
- DEPTH: 67'-2"

SEARCH ONLINE @ EPLANS.COM

Turret-style bay windows, an arched entryway and an elegant balustrade add timeless appeal to a remarkable facade, yet this refined exterior encompasses a very practical layout. Separated from the kitchen by an angled island, the great room features built-in shelves on both sides of the fireplace as well as French doors leading to the rear porch with a wet bar. Custom-style details include tray ceilings in the dining room and study/bedroom as well as columns in the foyer and master bath.

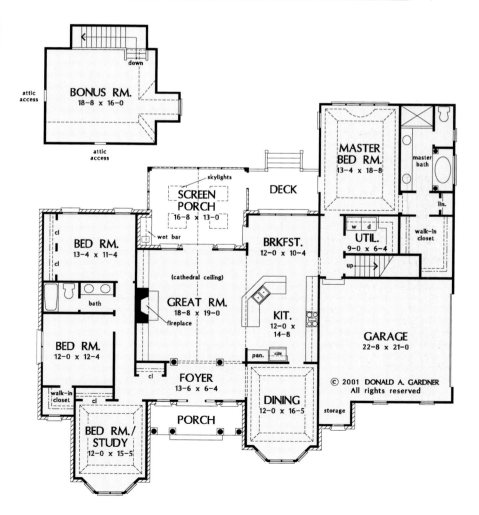

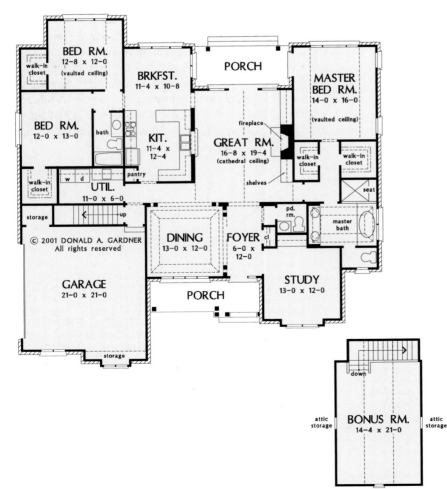

plan# HPT910086

- STYLE: TRADITIONAL
- SQUARE FOOTAGE: 2,330
- BONUS SPACE: 364 SQ. FT.
- BEDROOMS: 3
- BATHROOMS: 2½
- WIDTH: 62'-3"
- DEPTH: 60'-6"

SEARCH ONLINE @ EPLANS.COM

Quaint and simple, this country home with front dormers will charm the whole neighborhood. Inside, the foyer is flanked on either side by a formal dining room and a study. A cathedral ceiling enlarges the great room, which is warmed by a fireplace flanked by built-ins. The master suite is located to the right and includes two walk-in closets and a private bath.

TO ORDER BLUEPRINTS CALL TOLL FREE 1-800-521-6797

plan # HPT910087

- STYLE: TRADITIONAL
- FIRST FLOOR: 1,500 SQ. FT.
- SECOND FLOOR: 1,106 SQ. FT.
- TOTAL: 2,606 SQ. FT.
- BONUS SPACE: 366 SQ. FT.
- BEDROOMS: 4
- BATHROOMS: 2½
- WIDTH: 63'-3"
- DEPTH: 48'-1"

SEARCH ONLINE @ EPLANS.COM

Elegant and stately, the exterior of this traditional home features a Palladian-style window, which accents the front facade and floods the two-story foyer with light. The floor plan features open spaces with more room definition for those seeking a truly traditional design. Columns separate the formal living and dining rooms, while a bay window extends the breakfast area. French doors access the rear porch as well as connect the family room to the outdoors. Built-ins embrace the fireplace, and an angled counter allows the kitchen to take part in casual entertaining. The master bedroom features a tray ceiling; additional bedrooms share a full bath with the bonus room. Note the second-floor balcony.

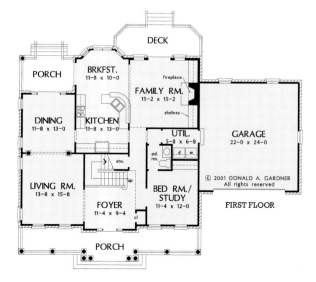

© 2002 Donald A. Gardner, Inc.

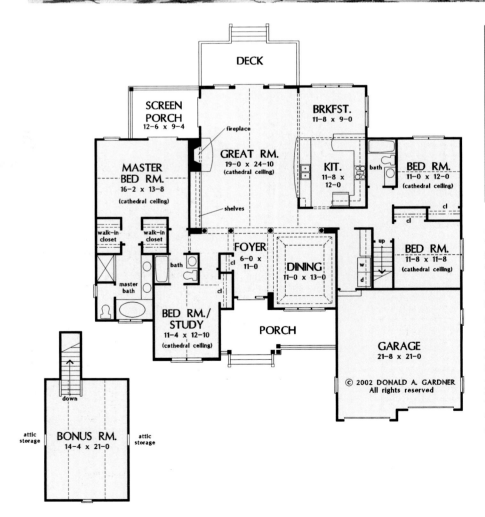

DECK

SCREEN PORCH
12-6 x 9-4

fireplace

GREAT RM.
19-0 x 24-10
(cathedral ceiling)

BRKFST.
11-8 x 9-0

KIT.
11-8 x 12-0

bath

BED RM.
11-0 x 12-0
(cathedral ceiling)

MASTER BED RM.
16-2 x 13-8
(cathedral ceiling)

shelves

cl

walk-in closet

walk-in closet

bath

FOYER
6-0 x 11-0

cl

DINING
11-0 x 13-0

up

w d

cl

BED RM.
11-8 x 11-8
(cathedral ceiling)

master bath

BED RM./ STUDY
11-4 x 12-10
(cathedral ceiling)

PORCH

GARAGE
21-8 x 21-0

© 2002 DONALD A. GARDNER
All rights reserved

down

attic storage

BONUS RM.
14-4 x 21-0

attic storage

plan # HPT910088

- STYLE: TRADITIONAL
- SQUARE FOOTAGE: 2,259
- BONUS SPACE: 352 SQ. FT.
- BEDROOMS: 4
- BATHROOMS: 3
- WIDTH: 64'-10"
- DEPTH: 59'-6"

SEARCH ONLINE @ EPLANS.COM

Luxurious features and gracious amenities fill this charming traditional design. The great room and all four of the bedrooms boast lofty cathedral ceilings; the great room also boasts a fireplace and access to the rear deck, while the master suite offers two walk-in closets and opens to a petite screened porch. The breakfast room, naturally illuminated by windows on both of its outer walls, provides a cozy space for family meals. Nearby, the kitchen includes plenty of counter space and easily serves the formal, tray-ceilinged dining room.

© 1999 Donald A. Gardner, Inc.

plan# HPT910089

- STYLE: TRADITIONAL
- FIRST FLOOR: 1,668 SQ. FT.
- SECOND FLOOR: 495 SQ. FT.
- TOTAL: 2,163 SQ. FT.
- BONUS SPACE: 327 SQ. FT.
- BEDROOMS: 4
- BATHROOMS: 3
- WIDTH: 52'-7"
- DEPTH: 50'-11"

SEARCH ONLINE @ EPLANS.COM

Four gables, a Palladian window and an admirable transom with a sunburst are eye-catching additions to this plan's exterior. On the first floor, rounded columns present the dining room, which also sports a tray ceiling. The vaulted great room accesses the rear deck and features a warming fireplace. Set at an angle, the kitchen's serving bar allows the cook to keep up with activities in both the breakfast and great rooms. The master suite includes a walk-in closet, tray ceiling and sumptuous bath. Note the triangular shape of the tub and separate shower. Upstairs, two family bedrooms share a full bath.

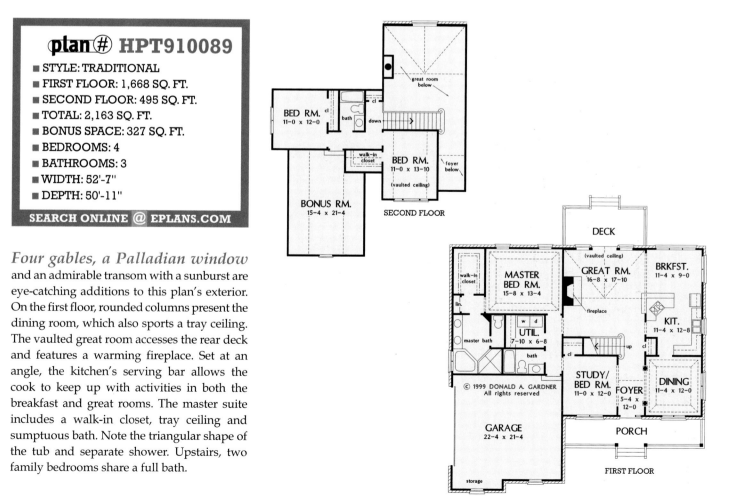

© 2002 Donald A. Gardner, Inc.

MASTER BED RM.
14-8 x 13-0

master bath

BED RM.
11-0 x 12-0

walk-in closet

bath

cl

lin.

cl

BED RM.
11-0 x 12-0

up

UTIL.
6-8 x
8-4

w

d

GREAT RM.
16-0 x 18-0
(cathedral ceiling)
fireplace

shelves

GARAGE
21-8 x 21-0

cl

FOYER
12-4 x 5-8

KIT.
9-0 x
15-0

pan.

PORCH

BRKFST.
9-0 x 9-0

PORCH

DINING
14-0 x 12-0

down

attic storage

attic storage

BONUS RM.
13-4 x 21-0

plan # HPT910090

- **STYLE:** TRADITIONAL
- **SQUARE FOOTAGE:** 1,707
- **BONUS SPACE:** 323 SQ. FT.
- **BEDROOMS:** 3
- **BATHROOMS:** 2
- **WIDTH:** 48'-6"
- **DEPTH:** 65'-6"

SEARCH ONLINE @ EPLANS.COM

An elegant Palladian window provides a focal point on the facade of this traditional home. The great room, with an entry that's defined by columns, includes a cathedral ceiling and fireplace flanked by built-in shelves. The nearby breakfast room adjoins the L-shaped kitchen, which easily serves the dining room. Sleeping quarters, located to the left of the plan, include two family bedrooms that share a full bath, as well as a master suite with a tray ceiling, a large walk-in closet and a private dual-vanity bath.

© 2002 Donald A. Gardner, Inc.

plan# HPT910091

- STYLE: TRADITIONAL
- SQUARE FOOTAGE: 1,606
- BONUS SPACE: 338 SQ. FT.
- BEDROOMS: 3
- BATHROOMS: 2
- WIDTH: 50'-0"
- DEPTH: 54'-0"

SEARCH ONLINE @ EPLANS.COM

Brick and horizontal siding blend perfectly on the facade of this traditional home, which is further decorated by a flower box and keystone lintel on the garage. An expansive great room, with a cathedral ceiling and access to the rear deck, shares a snack bar with the kitchen. A split-bedroom plan places the master suite to the rear of the home, where it offers a walk-in closet and a private bath with a double vanity and compartmented toilet. Two additional bedrooms sit to the left of the plan—one boasts a vaulted ceiling, and the other can double as a study.

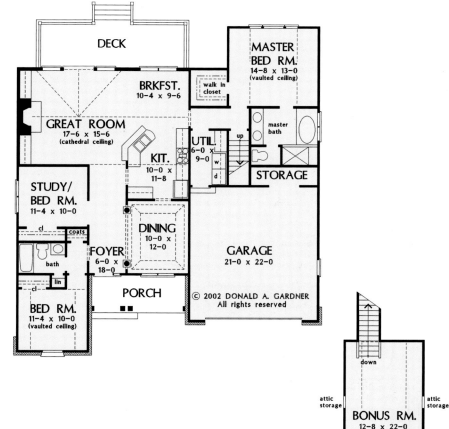

© 2002 Donald A. Gardner, Inc.

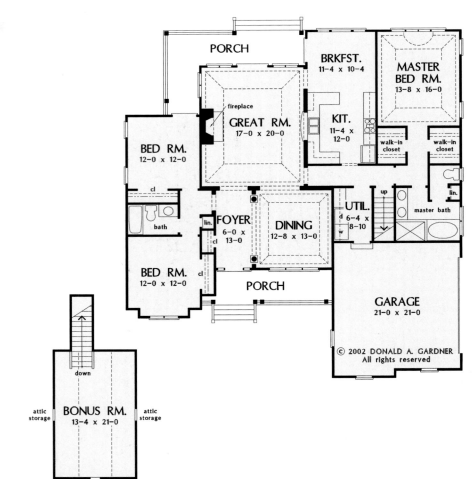

plan# HPT910092

- STYLE: TRADITIONAL
- SQUARE FOOTAGE: 1,955
- BONUS SPACE: 329 SQ. FT.
- BEDROOMS: 3
- BATHROOMS: 2
- WIDTH: 56'-0"
- DEPTH: 58'-4"

SEARCH ONLINE @ EPLANS.COM

A box-bay window adds classic style to this traditional design, and horizontal siding and a wide front porch provide country flair. Inside, two family bedrooms and a full bath sit to the left of the foyer; the rear bedroom opens to a wraparound porch. The great room and breakfast area, also with porch access, provide comfortable and casual gathering areas. The master suite, separated from the family bedrooms, boasts a tray ceiling, two walk-in closets, and a private bath with an elegant oval tub.

TO ORDER BLUEPRINTS CALL TOLL FREE 1-800-521-6797

© 2002 Donald A. Gardner, Inc.

plan# HPT910093

- STYLE: TRADITIONAL
- SQUARE FOOTAGE: 2,076
- BONUS SPACE: 351 SQ. FT.
- BEDROOMS: 4
- BATHROOMS: 2
- WIDTH: 55'-4"
- DEPTH: 60'-6"

SEARCH ONLINE @ EPLANS.COM

With a brick and siding exterior and beautiful box-bay windows, this home will complement any neighborhood. A fireplace and tray ceiling add a cozy element in the great room, and a window seat in the breakfast nook adds comfort and charm. The master suite is located on the far right, with dual walk-in closets and a fantastic bath. To the far left, three family bedrooms — or make one a study — all have outstanding features. Bonus space above the garage provides room to grow.

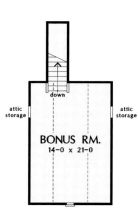

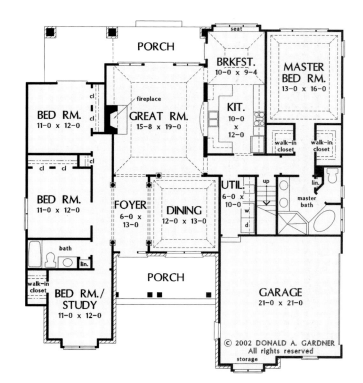

© 1999 Donald A. Gardner, Inc.

plan# HPT910094

- **STYLE:** TRADITIONAL
- **FIRST FLOOR:** 1,502 SQ. FT.
- **SECOND FLOOR:** 535 SQ. FT.
- **TOTAL:** 2,037 SQ. FT.
- **BONUS SPACE:** 275 SQ. FT.
- **BEDROOMS:** 3
- **BATHROOMS:** 2½
- **WIDTH:** 43'-0"
- **DEPTH:** 57'-6"

SEARCH ONLINE @ EPLANS.COM

This impressive home has an array of special features, yet it's cost-effective and easy-to-build for those on a limited budget. Tray ceilings elevate the bedroom/study, dining room and master bedroom. Turret bays illuminate the formal dining room and study. The great room features a cathedral ceiling and a striking fireplace. A smart angled counter is all that separates the great room, kitchen and bayed breakfast area. The master bedroom suite remains a private getaway from the rest of the home. Note the tub, large separate shower and double vanity.

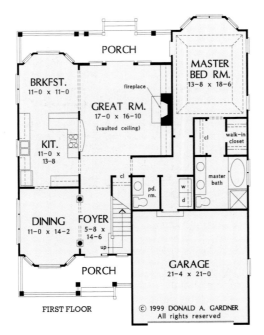

FIRST FLOOR

© 1999 DONALD A. GARDNER
All rights reserved

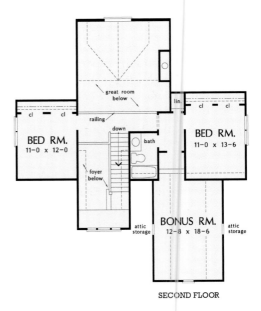

SECOND FLOOR

TO ORDER BLUEPRINTS CALL TOLL FREE 1-800-521-6797

plan # HPT910095

- STYLE: TRADITIONAL
- SQUARE FOOTAGE: 1,682
- BEDROOMS: 3
- BATHROOMS: 2½
- WIDTH: 48'-4"
- DEPTH: 64'-0"

SEARCH ONLINE @ EPLANS.COM

The hipped roof of this three-bedroom home protects a comfortable interior. A study or secondary bedroom opens to the right of the foyer and shares a full bath with an additional bedroom. Adorned with a tray ceiling, the master suite has all the amenities of a luxury home, including a walk-in closet, two-sink vanity, soaking tub, separate shower and compartmented toilet. The great room, with its beautiful fireplace and built-ins has views of the rear porch. Nearby, the dining room enjoys access to both the kitchen and the great room for easy entertaining.

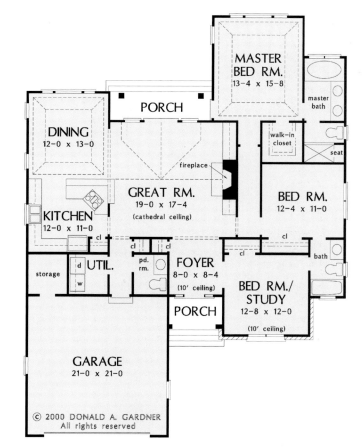

Enjoy the elegance of the stone-and-stucco exterior on this amenity-filled, four-bedroom home. An impressive fireplace features built-ins to each side within the great room. The secondary bedroom on the first floor—or make it a study—provides access to a full bath. The tray-ceilinged master suite includes a sumptuous bath, two walk-in closets and a bay window. Two secondary bedrooms, a bonus room and a full bath reside on the second floor.

plan # HPT910096

- **STYLE: TRADITIONAL**
- **FIRST FLOOR: 1,918 SQ. FT.**
- **SECOND FLOOR: 469 SQ. FT.**
- **TOTAL: 2,387 SQ. FT.**
- **BONUS SPACE: 374 SQ. FT.**
- **BEDROOMS: 4**
- **BATHROOMS: 3**
- **WIDTH: 73'-3"**
- **DEPTH: 43'-6"**

SEARCH ONLINE @ EPLANS.COM

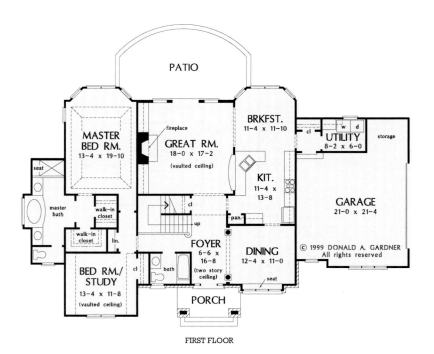

FIRST FLOOR

SECOND FLOOR

© 1998 Donald A. Gardner, Inc.

B. NATHAN

plan# HPT910097

- STYLE: TRADITIONAL
- FIRST FLOOR: 1,701 SQ. FT.
- SECOND FLOOR: 534 SQ. FT.
- TOTAL: 2,235 SQ. FT.
- BONUS SPACE: 274 SQ. FT.
- BEDROOMS: 3
- BATHROOMS: 2½
- WIDTH: 65'-11"
- DEPTH: 43'-5"

SEARCH ONLINE @ EPLANS.COM

Columns, gables, multi-pane windows and a stone and stucco exterior give this home its handsome appearance. The interior amenities are just as impressive. The formal rooms are to the right and left of the foyer with a powder room and coat closet down the hall. The family room, with a cathedral ceiling, fireplace, built-ins and access to the rear patio, is open to the breakfast room through a pair of decorative columns. On the opposite side of the plan, the master suite offers two walk-in closets and a compartmented bath. Two family bedrooms on the second floor share a bath and a loft that overlooks the family room.

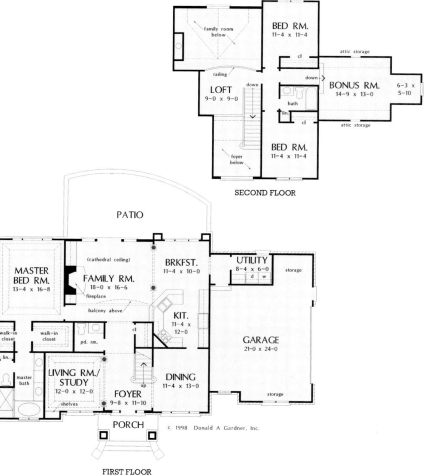

SECOND FLOOR

FIRST FLOOR

© 2001 Donald A. Gardner, Inc.

plan# HPT910098

- **STYLE:** TRADITIONAL
- **FIRST FLOOR:** 1,809 SQ. FT.
- **SECOND FLOOR:** 869 SQ. FT.
- **TOTAL:** 2,678 SQ. FT.
- **BONUS SPACE:** 320 SQ. FT.
- **BEDROOMS:** 4
- **BATHROOMS:** 3½
- **WIDTH:** 50'-7"
- **DEPTH:** 52'-7"

SEARCH ONLINE @ EPLANS.COM

With an elegant brick facade and a standing-seam roof that shelters the front porch, this traditional design brings back the stately homes of the past. Inside, the floor plan gives a nod to history in the parlor with a cathedral ceiling just to the left of the foyer; refined columns separate this room from the dining room. Less formal rooms—the kitchen, great room and breakfast area—all open to each other. The first-floor master suite includes a tray ceiling, walk-in closet and private bath. Upstairs, three bedrooms—one with a private bath—share a balcony that overlooks the great room.

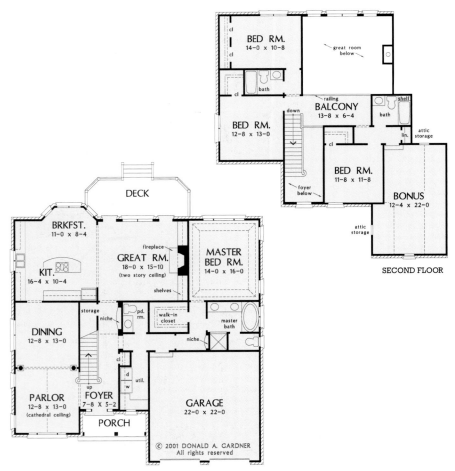

BED RM.
14-0 x 10-8

great room
below

bath

BED RM.
12-8 x 13-0

railing

BALCONY
13-8 x 6-4

shelf

bath

down

attic
storage

BED RM.
11-8 x 11-8

foyer
below

BONUS
12-4 x 22-0

attic
storage

SECOND FLOOR

DECK

BRKFST.
11-0 x 8-4

fireplace

GREAT RM.
18-0 x 15-10
(two story ceiling)

MASTER
BED RM.
14-0 x 16-0

KIT.
16-4 x 10-4

shelves

storage

niche

pd.
rm.

walk-in
closet

master
bath

DINING
12-8 x 13-0

niche

up

PARLOR
12-8 x 13-0
(cathedral ceiling)

FOYER
7-8 x 5-2

util.

GARAGE
22-0 x 22-0

PORCH

FIRST FLOOR

© 2002 Donald A. Gardner, Inc.

plan# HPT910099

- STYLE: TRADITIONAL
- FIRST FLOOR: 1,345 SQ. FT.
- SECOND FLOOR: 452 SQ. FT.
- TOTAL: 1,797 SQ. FT.
- BONUS SPACE: 349 SQ. FT.
- BEDROOMS: 3
- BATHROOMS: 2½
- WIDTH: 63'-0"
- DEPTH: 40'-0"

SEARCH ONLINE @ EPLANS.COM

Incorporating Old World style and elements, this house combines stone and stucco with gable peaks and arched windows for a stunning European facade. The grand portico leads to an open floor plan, which is equally impressive. Built-in cabinetry, French doors, and a fireplace enhance the great room; an angled counter separates the kitchen from the breakfast nook. The first-floor master suite is located in the quiet zone with no rooms above it. Upstairs, a balcony overlooks the great room. The bonus room features convenient second-floor access, and shares a full bath with two upstairs bathrooms.

SECOND FLOOR

great room below

BED RM.
11-0 x 11-0

attic storage

attic storage

railing

down

bath

lin.

cl

cl

shelf

BED RM.
11-0 x 11-0

attic storage

attic storage

BONUS RM.
11-8 x 22-0

foyer below

DECK

MASTER BED RM.
12-0 x 15-4

shelves
fireplace

GREAT RM.
15-4 x 17-10
(vaulted ceiling)

balcony above

BRKFST.
11-0 x 8-4

UTIL.
6-0 x
6-6

w
d

storage

KIT.
11-0 x
10-0

cl

walk-in closet

sto.

pd. rm.

cl

lin.

master bath

FOYER
9-2 x
9-6
(vaulted ceiling)

up

DINING
11-0 x 12-0

GARAGE
21-0 x 22-0

© 2002 DONALD A. GARDNER
All rights reserved

PORCH

storage

FIRST FLOOR

© 2001 Donald A. Gardner, Inc.

plan # HPT910100

- **STYLE:** TRADITIONAL
- **FIRST FLOOR:** 2,511 SQ. FT.
- **SECOND FLOOR:** 1,062 SQ. FT.
- **TOTAL:** 3,573 SQ. FT.
- **BONUS SPACE:** 465 SQ. FT.
- **BEDROOMS:** 4
- **BATHROOMS:** 3½
- **WIDTH:** 84'-11"
- **DEPTH:** 55'-11"

SEARCH ONLINE @ EPLANS.COM

An abundance of windows and an attractive brick facade enhance the exterior of this traditional two-story home. Inside, a study and formal dining room flank either side of the two-story foyer. Fireplaces warm both the great room and first-floor master suite. The suite also provides a separate sitting room, two walk-in closets and a private bath. The island kitchen extends into the breakfast room. The second floor features three additional family bedrooms, two baths and a bonus room fit for a home office.

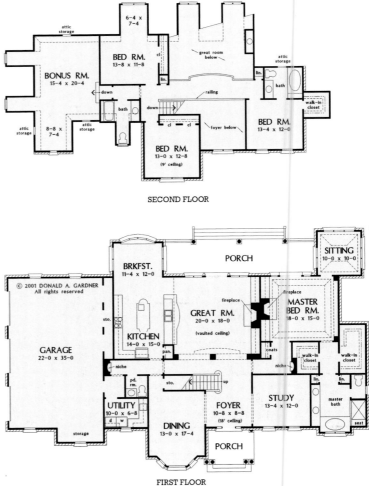

SECOND FLOOR

FIRST FLOOR

TO ORDER BLUEPRINTS CALL TOLL FREE 1-800-521-6797

© 2000 Donald A. Gardner, Inc.

This classic design has been restyled to bring more living enjoyment. Stately columns and dormers add distinction to the exterior. Inside, large rooms are the primary focus, giving families all the space they need. A sizeable powder room and open view of the great room greet the foyer. An open stair adds drama to this entry sequence without restricting the view through the house. The great room leads to the porch and to the spacious kitchen and breakfast nook with bay window. One special feature is the master suite with an angled garden tub, double vanity, large shower and private toilet. Other significant highlights include a bonus room and a notable storage area off the garage.

plan # HPT910101

- STYLE: TRADITIONAL
- FIRST FLOOR: 985 SQ. FT.
- SECOND FLOOR: 870 SQ. FT.
- TOTAL: 1,855 SQ. FT.
- BONUS SPACE: 331 SQ. FT.
- BEDROOMS: 3
- BATHROOMS: 2½
- WIDTH: 53'-5"
- DEPTH: 36'-2"

SEARCH ONLINE @ EPLANS.COM

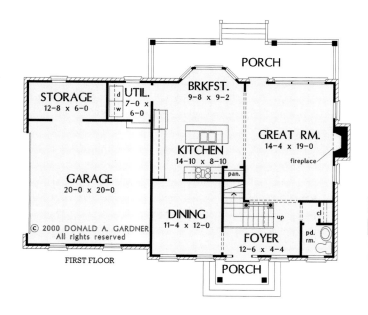

FIRST FLOOR

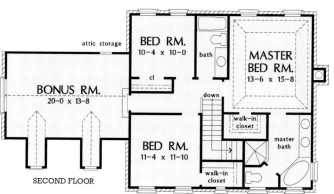

SECOND FLOOR

© 2002 Donald A. Gardner, Inc.

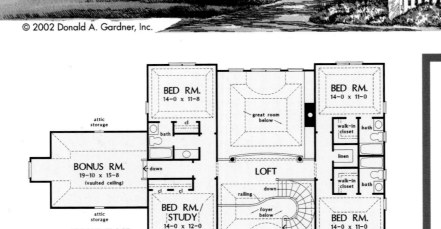

BED RM.
14-0 x 11-8

BED RM.
14-0 x 11-0

attic
storage

BONUS RM.
19-10 x 15-8
(vaulted ceiling)

great room
below

walk-in
closet

bath

bath

down

LOFT

linen

attic
storage

BED RM./
STUDY
14-0 x 12-0

cl — cl

railing

down

foyer
below

walk-in
closet

bath

SECOND FLOOR

BED RM.
14-0 x 11-0

plan # HPT910102

- STYLE: TRADITIONAL
- FIRST FLOOR: 2,062 SQ. FT.
- SECOND FLOOR: 1,279 SQ. FT.
- TOTAL: 3,341 SQ. FT.
- BONUS SPACE: 386 SQ. FT.
- BEDROOMS: 5
- BATHROOMS: 4½
- WIDTH: 73'-8"
- DEPTH: 50'-0"

SEARCH ONLINE @ EPLANS.COM

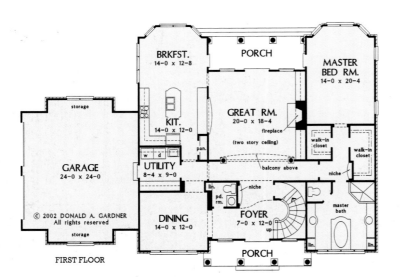

BRKFST.
14-0 x 12-8

PORCH

MASTER
BED RM.
14-0 x 20-4

storage

KIT.
14-0 x 12-0

GREAT RM.
20-0 x 18-4

fireplace

(two story ceiling)

walk-in
closet

walk-in
closet

GARAGE
24-0 x 24-0

w d

UTILITY
8-4 x 9-0

pan.

balcony above

niche

© 2002 DONALD A. GARDNER
All rights reserved

lin.

niche

pd.
rm.

master
bath

storage

DINING
14-0 x 12-0

FOYER
7-0 x 12-0

up

lin.

lin.

FIRST FLOOR

PORCH

A hipped roofline, a decorative second-story balcony and stone accents provide touches of European style on this traditional design. Inside, the foyer is enhanced by an elegant curved staircase, an art niche and a powder room; the formal dining room sits to the left. Columns define the entrance to the spacious central great room, which also includes a fireplace, built-ins and access to the rear porch. Bay windows allow natural light to fill the breakfast area and master bedroom. Upstairs, four family bedrooms — three with private baths — boast unique ceiling treatments. A cozy loft area overlooks the great room.

Plan HPT910124; see page 156 for details.

CABINS & COTTAGES

Find open, flowing floor plans and an appreciation for the outdoors in this collection of quaint cabins and cottages.

This cottage combines stone, siding, and cedar shake to create striking curb appeal. The interior features an open floor plan with high ceilings, columns and bay windows to visually expand space. Built-in cabinetry, a fireplace and a kitchen pass-through highlight and add convenience to the great room. The master suite features a tray ceiling in the bedroom and a bath with garden tub, separate shower, dual vanities, and a walk-in closet. On the opposite side of the home another bedroom could be used as a second master suite. Above the garage, a bonus room provides ample storage and space to grow.

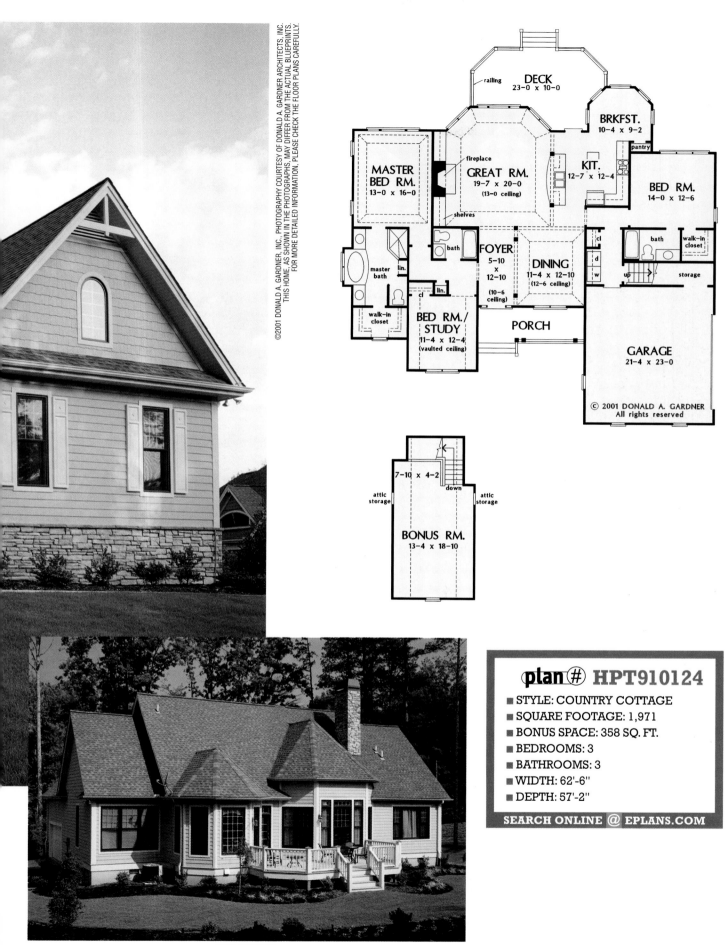

DECK
23-0 x 10-0

railing

BRKFST.
10-4 x 9-2

pantry

MASTER BED RM.
13-0 x 16-0

fireplace

GREAT RM.
19-7 x 20-0
(13-0 ceiling)

KIT.
12-7 x 12-4

BED RM.
14-0 x 12-6

shelves

bath

FOYER
5-10 x 12-10
(10-6 ceiling)

DINING
11-4 x 12-10
(12-6 ceiling)

master bath

lin.

bath

walk-in closet

cl

lin.

cl

walk-in closet

up

storage

BED RM./ STUDY
11-4 x 12-4
(vaulted ceiling)

PORCH

GARAGE
21-4 x 23-0

7-10 x 4-2

down

attic storage

attic storage

BONUS RM.
13-4 x 18-10

plan# HPT910124

- **STYLE:** COUNTRY COTTAGE
- **SQUARE FOOTAGE:** 1,971
- **BONUS SPACE:** 358 SQ. FT.
- **BEDROOMS:** 3
- **BATHROOMS:** 3
- **WIDTH:** 62'-6"
- **DEPTH:** 57'-2"

SEARCH ONLINE @ EPLANS.COM

REAR EXTERIOR

This economical, rustic, three-bedroom plan sports a relaxing country image with both front and back covered porches. The openness of the expansive great room to the kitchen/dining areas and the loft/study areas is reinforced with a shared cathedral ceiling for impressive space. The first floor provides two bedrooms, a full bath and a utility area. The master suite upstairs offers a walk-in closet and a whirlpool tub.

Quote One®

Cost to build? See page 186
to order complete cost estimate
to build this house in your area!

plan# HPT910105

- STYLE: COUNTRY COTTAGE
- FIRST FLOOR: 1,027 SQ. FT.
- SECOND FLOOR: 580 SQ. FT.
- TOTAL: 1,607 SQ. FT.
- BEDROOMS: 3
- BATHROOMS: 2
- WIDTH: 37'-4"
- DEPTH: 44'-8"

SEARCH ONLINE @ EPLANS.COM

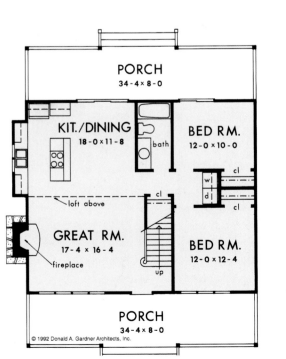

FIRST FLOOR

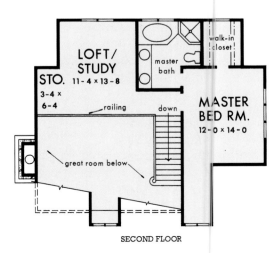

SECOND FLOOR

TO ORDER BLUEPRINTS CALL TOLL FREE 1-800-521-6797

© 1994 Donald A. Gardner Architects, Inc.

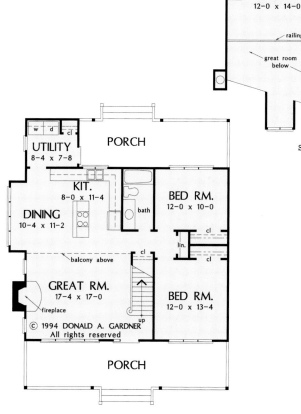

plan # HPT910106

- STYLE: COUNTRY COTTAGE
- FIRST FLOOR: 1,100 SQ. FT.
- SECOND FLOOR: 584 SQ. FT.
- TOTAL: 1,684 SQ. FT.
- BEDROOMS: 3
- BATHROOMS: 2
- WIDTH: 36'-8"
- DEPTH: 45'-0"

SEARCH ONLINE @ EPLANS.COM

A relaxing country image projects from the front and rear covered porches of this rustic three-bedroom home. Open planning extends to the great room, the dining room, and the efficient kitchen. A shared cathedral ceiling creates an impressive space. Completing the first floor are two family bedrooms, a full bath, and a handy utility area. The second floor contains the master suite featuring a spacious walk-in closet and a master bath with a whirlpool tub and a separate corner shower. A generous loft/study overlooks the great room below.

LOFT/STUDY 12-0 x 14-0

master bath

walk-in closet

railing

down

great room below

MASTER BED RM. 12-0 x 14-0

attic storage

SECOND FLOOR

UTILITY 8-4 x 7-8

PORCH

KIT. 8-0 x 11-4

bath

BED RM. 12-0 x 10-0

DINING 10-4 x 11-2

cl

lin.

cl

balcony above

GREAT RM. 17-4 x 17-0

fireplace

© 1994 DONALD A. GARDNER
All rights reserved

up

BED RM. 12-0 x 13-4

PORCH

FIRST FLOOR

©1998 Donald A. Gardner, Inc.

Gable treatments along with stone and horizontal siding give a definite country flavor to this two-story home. The formal dining room is accented with decorative columns that define its perimeter. The great room boasts a fireplace, built-ins and a magnificent view of the backyard beyond the rear porch. The master suite boasts two walk-in closets and a private bath. Two bedrooms share a full bath on the second floor.

plan# HPT910107

- STYLE: COUNTRY COTTAGE
- FIRST FLOOR: 1,336 SQ. FT.
- SECOND FLOOR: 523 SQ. FT.
- TOTAL: 1,859 SQ. FT.
- BONUS SPACE: 225 SQ. FT.
- BEDROOMS: 3
- BATHROOMS: 2½
- WIDTH: 45'-0"
- DEPTH: 53'-0"

SEARCH ONLINE @ EPLANS.COM

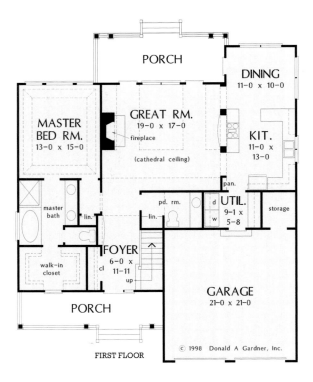

FIRST FLOOR

© 1998 Donald A Gardner, Inc.

SECOND FLOOR

TO ORDER BLUEPRINTS CALL TOLL FREE 1-800-521-6797

plan # HPT910108

- STYLE: COUNTRY COTTAGE
- SQUARE FOOTAGE: 1,559
- BEDROOMS: 3
- BATHROOMS: 2
- WIDTH: 54'-4"
- DEPTH: 52'-0"

SEARCH ONLINE @ EPLANS.COM

Both formal and informal rooms are found in this one-story country home—even though it contains less square footage. The foyer opens to a formal dining room to the right and a great room with a cathedral ceiling straight ahead. The breakfast room and kitchen lie just to the right of the great room. Family bedrooms on the left side of the plan share a full hall bath. The master suite is tucked in behind the two-car garage and accesses the rear deck, as does the great room.

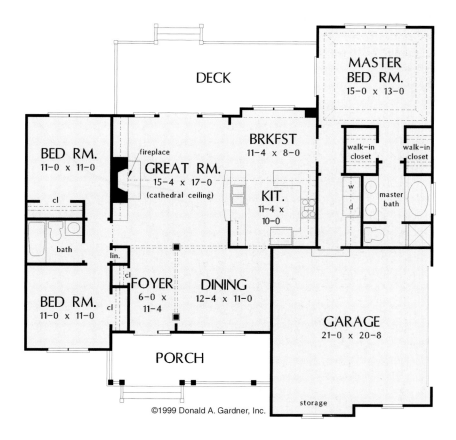

©1999 Donald A. Gardner, Inc.

This nostalgic bungalow's facade is enhanced by a charming gable, twin dormers and a wrapping front porch. Bay windows enlarge both the dining room and the master bedroom and the vaulted great room receives additional light from a front clerestory window. The kitchen features a practical design and includes a handy pantry and ample cabinets. A nearby utility room boasts a sink and additional cabinet and countertop space. Located on the first floor for convenience, the master suite enjoys a private bath and a walk-in closet. Upstairs, two more bedrooms and a generous bonus room share a full bath.

plan # HPT910109

- STYLE: COUNTRY COTTAGE
- FIRST FLOOR: 1,293 SQ. FT.
- SECOND FLOOR: 528 SQ. FT.
- TOTAL: 1,821 SQ. FT.
- BONUS SPACE: 355 SQ. FT.
- BEDROOMS: 3
- BATHROOMS: 2½
- WIDTH: 48'-8"
- DEPTH: 50'-0"

SEARCH ONLINE @ EPLANS.COM

FIRST FLOOR

SECOND FLOOR

TO ORDER BLUEPRINTS CALL TOLL FREE 1-800-521-6797

plan # HPT910110

- **STYLE: COUNTRY COTTAGE**
- **SQUARE FOOTAGE: 1,671**
- **BONUS SPACE: 348 SQ. FT.**
- **BEDROOMS: 3**
- **BATHROOMS: 2**
- **WIDTH: 50'-8"**
- **DEPTH: 52'-4"**

SEARCH ONLINE @ EPLANS.COM

The front porch of this home offers sanctuary from the elements and welcoming charm. To the right, the formal dining room features a tray ceiling and pocket-door access to the kitchen. To the left, a study or guest bedroom also features a tray ceiling and accesses a full bath. The great room sits at the center with a fireplace, built-ins, a cathedral ceiling and rear-deck access. With the breakfast area soaking up natural light from its many windows and the gourmet kitchen just steps away, the family will enjoy ease of service and a casual atmosphere. The master suite offers a cathedral ceiling, a spacious walk-in closet and a bath with dual vanities.

© 1998 Donald A. Gardner, Inc.

Soaring gables make this narrow-lot design larger than its modest square footage on the outside, while cathedral and tray ceilings enhance interior spaciousness. A flowing floor plan positions the great room, dining room and kitchen in convenient proximity. The great room features a fireplace with flanking built-in cabinets and bookshelves, access to the back porch and a pass-through to the efficient kitchen. A generous bonus room with an adjacent storage area provides ample room to grow.

plan# HPT910111

- **STYLE: COUNTRY COTTAGE**
- **SQUARE FOOTAGE: 1,481**
- **BONUS SPACE: 643 SQ. FT.**
- **BEDROOMS: 3**
- **BATHROOMS: 2**
- **WIDTH: 42'-4"**
- **DEPTH: 65'-10"**

SEARCH ONLINE @ EPLANS.COM

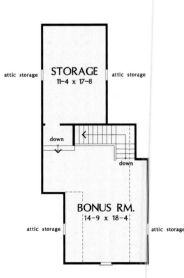

plan # HPT910112

- STYLE: COUNTRY COTTAGE
- SQUARE FOOTAGE: 1,399
- BONUS SPACE: 296 SQ. FT.
- BEDROOMS: 3
- BATHROOMS: 2
- WIDTH: 58'-0"
- DEPTH: 44'-4"

SEARCH ONLINE @ EPLANS.COM

Open gables, a covered porch and shuttered windows bring out the country flavor of this three-bedroom home. Inside, the great room enjoys a cathedral ceiling and a fireplace. Decorative columns set off the formal dining room, which is only steps away from the well-outfitted kitchen. Here, a window sink, a pantry and a cooktop island overlooking the great room make an ideal food-preparation environment. Two family bedrooms located to the right of the plan share a full bath. The secluded master suite is highlighted by dual vanities, a compartmented shower and toilet, separate tub, walk-in closet and cathedral ceiling.

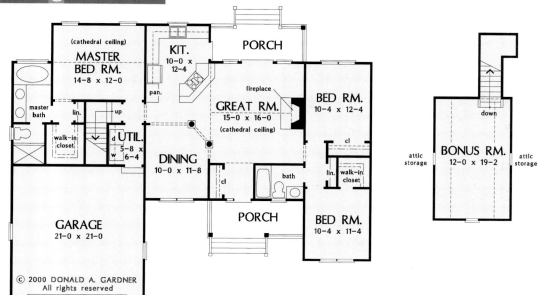

An arched window in a center front-facing gable lends style and beauty to the facade of this three-bedroom home. An open common area features a great room with a cathedral ceiling, a formal dining room with a tray ceiling, a functional kitchen and an informal breakfast area that separates the master suite from the secondary bedrooms for privacy. The master suite provides a dramatic vaulted ceiling, access to the back porch and abundant closet space. Access to a versatile bonus room is near the master bedroom.

plan# HPT910113

- STYLE: COUNTRY COTTAGE
- SQUARE FOOTAGE: 1,882
- BONUS SPACE: 363 SQ. FT.
- BEDROOMS: 3
- BATHROOMS: 2½
- WIDTH: 61'-4"
- DEPTH: 55'-0"

SEARCH ONLINE @ EPLANS.COM

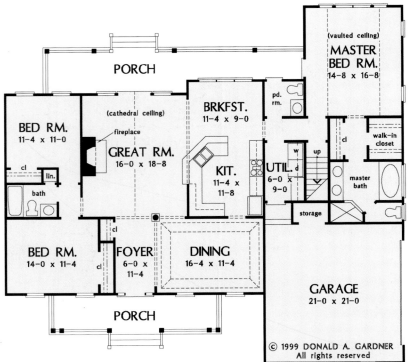

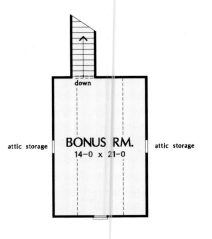

TO ORDER BLUEPRINTS CALL TOLL FREE 1-800-521-6797

plan# HPT910114

- **STYLE:** COUNTRY COTTAGE
- **SQUARE FOOTAGE:** 1,596
- **BONUS SPACE:** 367 SQ. FT.
- **BEDROOMS:** 3
- **BATHROOMS:** 2
- **WIDTH:** 57'-6"
- **DEPTH:** 58'-2"

SEARCH ONLINE @ EPLANS.COM

Vertical and horizontal siding mix with a generous front porch for a charming country facade on this modest three-bedroom home. Cathedral ceilings add volume to the great room and master bedroom, while the dining room is enhanced by an elegant tray ceiling. The great room also features built-in bookshelves on either side of the fireplace and access to the relaxing screened porch. The front bedroom/study is flex space with an optional door location depending on its use. Note this home's generous bonus room.

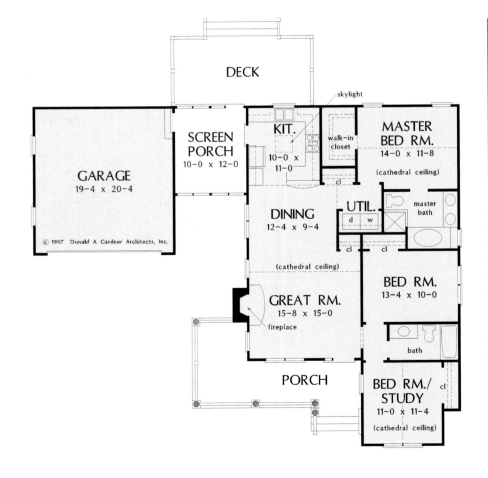

DECK

skylight

SCREEN PORCH
10-0 x 12-0

KIT.
10-0 x 11-0

walk-in closet

MASTER BED RM.
14-0 x 11-8
(cathedral ceiling)

GARAGE
19-4 x 20-4

© 1997 Donald A Gardner Architects, Inc.

DINING
12-4 x 9-4

UTIL.
d   w

cl   cl

master bath

(cathedral ceiling)

GREAT RM.
15-8 x 15-0
fireplace

BED RM.
13-4 x 10-0

bath

PORCH

BED RM./ STUDY
11-0 x 11-4
(cathedral ceiling)

cl

plan# HPT910115

- STYLE: COUNTRY COTTAGE
- SQUARE FOOTAGE: 1,246
- BEDROOMS: 3
- BATHROOMS: 2
- WIDTH: 60'-0"
- DEPTH: 48'-0"

SEARCH ONLINE @ EPLANS.COM

Open living spaces allow an easy flow in this gracious country cottage, and vaulted ceilings add volume. The front porch wraps slightly, giving the illusion of a larger home, and a cathedral ceiling maximizes space in the open great room and dining room. The kitchen features a center skylight, breakfast bar and screened-porch access. Two bedrooms share a bath near the entry, while the master suite enjoys a private location at the back of the plan. Luxuriate in the master bath with its separate shower, garden tub and twin-sink vanity.

© 1999 Donald A. Gardner, Inc.

plan# HPT910116

- STYLE: COUNTRY COTTAGE
- SQUARE FOOTAGE: 1,590
- BONUS SPACE: 425 SQ. FT.
- BEDROOMS: 3
- BATHROOMS: 2
- WIDTH: 55'-0"
- DEPTH: 59'-10"

SEARCH ONLINE @ EPLANS.COM

A cozy front porch and gables create warmth and style for this economical home with an open floor plan and a sizable bonus room. The openness of the great room, dining room, kitchen and breakfast room increases spaciousness. Additional volume is created by the cathedral ceiling that tops the great room and breakfast area, while a tray ceiling adds distinction and elegance to the formal dining room. Living space is extended to the outdoors by way of a rear deck. The master suite is separated from family bedrooms for parental privacy and features a luxurious bath with plenty of closet space. Two family bedrooms share a hall bath on the opposite side of the home.

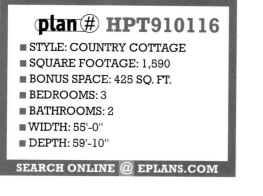

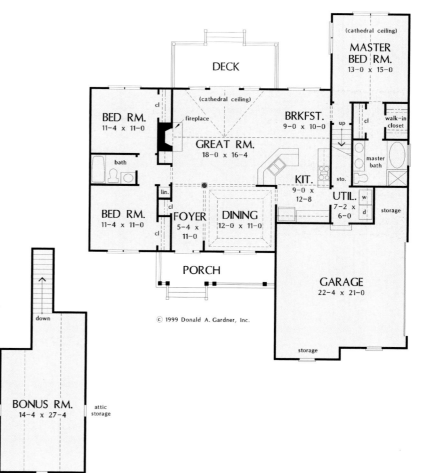

© 1999 Donald A. Gardner, Inc.

© 2000 Donald A. Gardner, Inc.

B. NATHAN

plan# HPT910117

- **STYLE:** COUNTRY COTTAGE
- **SQUARE FOOTAGE:** 1,593
- **BONUS SPACE:** 332 SQ. FT.
- **BEDROOMS:** 3
- **BATHROOMS:** 2
- **WIDTH:** 50'-0"
- **DEPTH:** 54'-0"

SEARCH ONLINE @ EPLANS.COM

The vaulted ceiling in the great room and tray ceiling in the dining room add richness to this charming, indulgent cottage design. Decorative columns define the dining room; the kitchen, breakfast area and great room are one large, open area. The great room features a fireplace, built-ins and access to the rear deck. The arch in the master bedroom is tray ceiling tops a triple window; note the shower seat in the master bath. Two family bedrooms—one can double as a study—sit to the front of the plan.

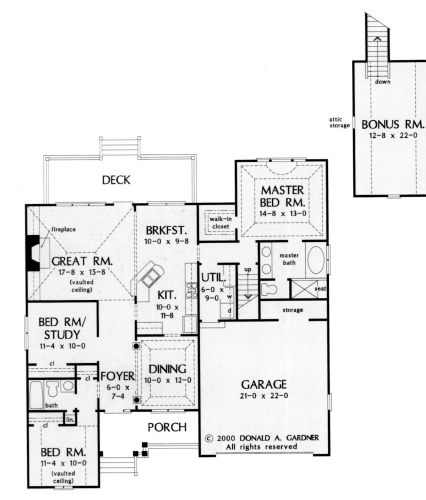

BONUS RM.
12-8 x 22-0

down
attic storage   attic storage

DECK

fireplace

BRKFST.
10-0 x 9-8

MASTER BED RM.
14-8 x 13-0

walk-in closet

GREAT RM.
17-8 x 15-8
(vaulted ceiling)

master bath

KIT.
10-0 x 11-8

UTIL.
6-0 x 9-0

up

seat

storage

BED RM/ STUDY
11-4 x 10-0

cl

FOYER
6-0 x 7-4

DINING
10-0 x 12-0

GARAGE
21-0 x 22-0

cl
bath
lin.

BED RM.
11-4 x 10-0
(vaulted ceiling)

PORCH

TO ORDER BLUEPRINTS CALL TOLL FREE 1-800-521-6797

© 1997 Donald A. Gardner Architects, Inc.

plan# HPT910118

- STYLE: COUNTRY COTTAGE
- SQUARE FOOTAGE: 1,770
- BONUS SPACE: 401 SQ. FT.
- BEDROOMS: 3
- BATHROOMS: 2
- WIDTH: 54'-0"
- DEPTH: 57'-8"

SEARCH ONLINE @ EPLANS.COM

The open floor plan of this delightful design combines the great room, kitchen and dining room for today's family. With light drawn through two rear dormers, the great room boasts a cathedral ceiling and a fireplace with flanking built-ins. Impress guests with this breathtaking dining room with an octagonal tray ceiling and light-filled bay windows. Tray ceilings also adorn the master bedroom and one of two secondary bedrooms. Escape to the relaxing master suite with a private bath oasis featuring a garden tub and two vanity sinks set in a bay window. An optional bonus room gives flexibility to this amazing home.

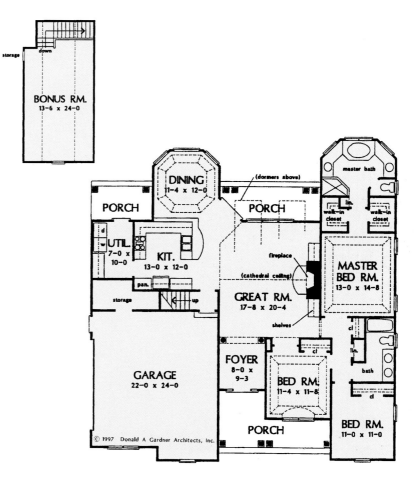

© 2000 Donald A. Gardner, Inc.

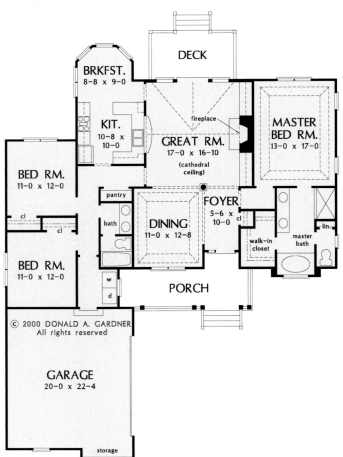

DECK

BRKFST.
8-8 x 9-0

KIT.
10-8 x
10-0

fireplace

GREAT RM.
17-0 x 16-10
(cathedral
ceiling)

MASTER
BED RM.
13-0 x 17-0

BED RM.
11-0 x 12-0

cl

cl

pantry

bath

DINING
11-0 x 12-8

FOYER
5-6 x
10-0

cl

lin.

BED RM.
11-0 x 12-0

walk-in
closet

master
bath

w
d

PORCH

GARAGE
20-0 x 22-4

storage

plan# HPT910119

- STYLE: COUNTRY COTTAGE
- SQUARE FOOTAGE: 1,684
- BEDROOMS: 3
- BATHROOMS: 2
- WIDTH: 53'-4"
- DEPTH: 66'-10"

SEARCH ONLINE @ EPLANS.COM

This design offers a facade with nested gables, twin dormers and a welcoming covered entry with enough space to accommodate a porch swing for romantic interludes under the stars. The highlight of the interior is the magnificent great room where an intricate cathedral ceiling complements the window wall, and the fireplace is framed by built-ins. Set to the right, the luxurious master suite offers privacy. To the left, the kitchen adjoins the breakfast nook. Two family bedrooms share a full bath on the far left where the hall leads past the laundry area to the two-car garage.

© 2002 Donald A. Gardner, Inc.

plan# HPT910120

- **STYLE: COUNTRY COTTAGE**
- **FIRST FLOOR: 1,834 SQ. FT.**
- **SECOND FLOOR: 681 SQ. FT.**
- **TOTAL: 2,515 SQ. FT.**
- **BONUS SPACE: 365 SQ. FT.**
- **BEDROOMS: 3**
- **BATHROOMS: 3½**
- **WIDTH: 50'-8"**
- **DEPTH: 66'-8"**

Stone, shingles, and three shed dormers give pleasantly rustic touches to this cottage's exterior. The formal dining room, to the right of the foyer, includes a tray ceiling, and the more casual kitchen and breakfast area share a snack bar. With its fireplace, built-in shelves and access to the rear porch, the great room is a perfect blend of formal and informal. A luxurious master suite with two walk-in closets and a private bath resides on the first floor; upstairs, two family bedrooms—each with a private bath—join a spacious bonus room.

SECOND FLOOR

FIRST FLOOR

© 2002 DONALD A. GARDNER
All rights reserved

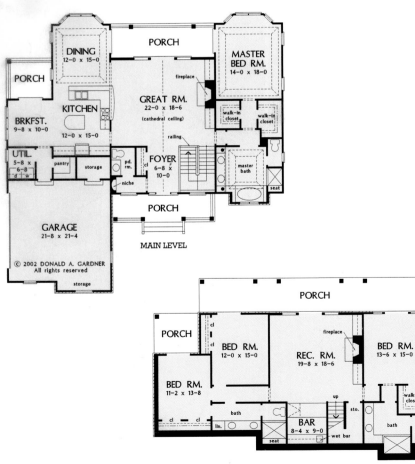

© 2002 Donald A. Gardner, Inc.

DINING
12-0 x 15-0

PORCH

MASTER BED RM.
14-0 x 18-0

PORCH

KITCHEN
12-0 x 15-0

fireplace

GREAT RM.
22-0 x 18-6
(cathedral ceiling)

walk-in closet

walk-in closet

BRKFST.
9-8 x 10-0

railing

UTIL.
5-8 x 6-8
w d

pantry

storage

pd. rm.

FOYER
6-8 x 10-0

master bath

niche

seat

GARAGE
21-8 x 21-4

PORCH

© 2002 DONALD A. GARDNER
All rights reserved

storage

MAIN LEVEL

PORCH

PORCH

cl
cl

BED RM.
12-0 x 15-0

fireplace

REC. RM.
19-8 x 18-6

BED RM.
13-6 x 15-0

BED RM.
11-2 x 13-8

up

sto.

walk-in closet

cl   cl

bath

lin.

BAR
8-4 x 9-0

wet bar

bath

seat

LOWER LEVEL

---

plan # HPT910129

- **STYLE:** COUNTRY COTTAGE
- **MAIN LEVEL:** 1,600 SQ. FT.
- **LOWER LEVEL:** 1,797 SQ. FT.
- **TOTAL:** 3,397 SQ. FT.
- **BEDROOMS:** 4
- **BATHROOMS:** 3½
- **WIDTH:** 59'-0"
- **DEPTH:** 59'-4"

SEARCH ONLINE @ EPLANS.COM

Stone accents and a shingled roof add Craftsman appeal to this charming cottage. A welcoming covered porch will usher you into the foyer: to the right, a railed staircase leads down to three bedrooms — one with a private bath — and a recreation room with a wet bar. Follow the vault of a cathedral ceiling from the foyer to the great room and admire the warming hearth and rear views. The country island kitchen easily serves the breakfast and dining rooms; both host abundant sunlight and porch access. Secluded in the right wing, the master suite includes a sunny bay window, dual walk-in closets and a decadent bath.

© 2001 Donald A. Gardner, Inc.

plan # HPT910121

- **STYLE: COUNTRY COTTAGE**
- **SQUARE FOOTAGE: 1,610**
- **BONUS SPACE: 353 SQ. FT.**
- **BEDROOMS: 3**
- **BATHROOMS: 2**
- **WIDTH: 49'-11"**
- **DEPTH: 55'-1"**

SEARCH ONLINE @ EPLANS.COM

Flower boxes, shuttered windows and a cozy front porch lend a country feel to this brick traditional home. Inside, a bedroom/study sits to the left of the foyer; directly ahead, the great room opens to a small side porch and features a fireplace flanked by built-in bookshelves. An efficient kitchen easily serves the dining room, which boasts a tray ceiling. Sleeping quarters to the left of the plan include a master suite, with a large walk-in closet and private bath, and one family bedroom with access to a nearby full bath. Upstairs, a bonus room can serve as a third bedroom, recreation room or game room.

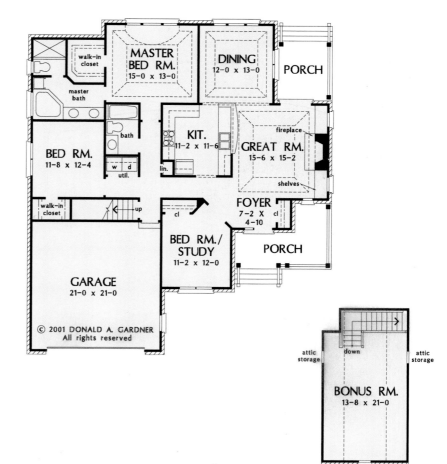

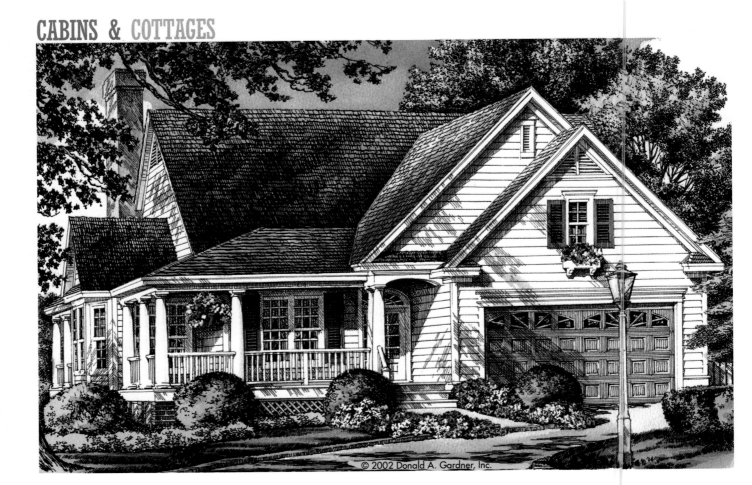

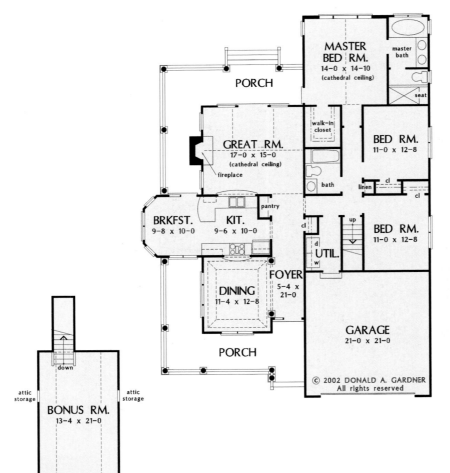

plan# HPT910122

- **STYLE: COUNTRY COTTAGE**
- **SQUARE FOOTAGE: 1,700**
- **BONUS SPACE: 333 SQ. FT.**
- **BEDROOMS: 3**
- **BATHROOMS: 2**
- **WIDTH: 49'-0"**
- **DEPTH: 65'-4"**

SEARCH ONLINE @ EPLANS.COM

Two wraparound porches lend a country feel to this cozy cottage. The formal dining room, with plenty of windows and a tray ceiling, sits to the left of the foyer; straight ahead, the great room boasts a cathedral ceiling, a fireplace and access to the rear porch. A cathedral ceiling also enriches the master bedroom, which boasts a walk-in closet and a private bath with a separate tub and shower. Two family bedrooms share a full hall bath, and are located conveniently close to the utility room.

TO ORDER BLUEPRINTS CALL TOLL FREE 1-800-521-6797

© 2002 Donald A. Gardner, Inc.

plan# HPT910123

- **STYLE:** COUNTRY COTTAGE
- **SQUARE FOOTAGE:** 1,457
- **BONUS SPACE:** 341 SQ. FT.
- **BEDROOMS:** 3
- **BATHROOMS:** 2
- **WIDTH:** 50'-4"
- **DEPTH:** 46'-4"

SEARCH ONLINE @ EPLANS.COM

Poised and cozy, this traditional home features a split-bedroom plan, along with half-circle transoms and tall gables on the front elevation. Above the convenient front-entry garage is a versatile bonus room for expansion. Economical and builder-friendly, the floor plan is family efficient and has a variety of custom-styled touches, such as tray ceilings in the dining room and master bedroom. The cathedral kitchen is convenient to the great room, which is highlighted by a cathedral ceiling, fireplace and French doors that lead to the rear porch. The master suite is complete with a walk-in closet and master bath; an additional bedroom and study/bedroom are located on the opposite side of the house and are separated by a full bath.

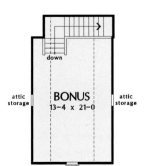

© 1997 Donald A. Gardner Architects, Inc.

B. NATHAN

This rustic retreat is updated with contemporary angles, and packs a lot of living into a small space. The covered front porch leads to a welcoming foyer. The beamed-ceiling great room opens directly ahead and features a fireplace, a wall of windows and access to the screened porch (with its own fireplace!). A highly efficient island kitchen is sure to please with tons of counter and cabinet space. Two family bedrooms, sharing a full bath, are located on one end of the plan while the master suite is secluded for complete privacy at the other end.

plan # HPT910104

- **STYLE: COUNTRY COTTAGE**
- **SQUARE FOOTAGE: 1,680**
- **BEDROOMS: 3**
- **BATHROOMS: 2**
- **WIDTH: 62'-8"**
- **DEPTH: 59'-10"**

SEARCH ONLINE @ EPLANS.COM

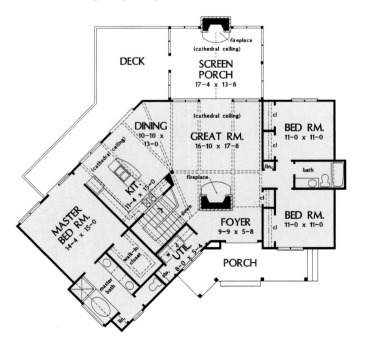

plan # HPT910125

- **STYLE: COUNTRY COTTAGE**
- **SQUARE FOOTAGE: 1,952**
- **BONUS SPACE: 339 SQ. FT.**
- **BEDROOMS: 3**
- **BATHROOMS: 2**
- **WIDTH: 50'-0"**
- **DEPTH: 60'-0"**

SEARCH ONLINE @ EPLANS.COM

As at home in a development as it is on an orchard, this design combines country charm with Craftsman appeal. A Palladian-style window fills the study/bedroom with light, while a stone wall and cozy front porch recall times past. A sole column and tray ceiling distinguish the dining room that opens to a great room, which features French doors to the rear porch and a striking two-room fireplace. An angled counter separates the kitchen from the great room and breakfast nook. With a master bath, two full additional baths, an optional study/bedroom and a bonus room, this home has plenty of space for growing families.

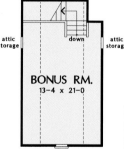

BONUS RM.
13-4 x 21-0

attic storage down attic storag

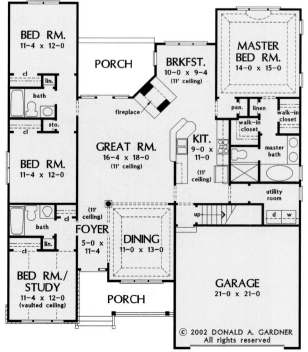

BED RM.
11-4 x 12-0

PORCH

BRKFST.
10-0 x 9-4
(11' ceiling)

MASTER BED RM.
14-0 x 15-0

bath

fireplace

pan. linen

walk-in closet

walk-in closet

GREAT RM.
16-4 x 18-0
(11' ceiling)

BED RM.
11-4 x 12-0

KIT.
9-0 x 11-0

(11' ceiling)

master bath

utility room

bath

FOYER
5-0 x 11-4

(11' ceiling)

DINING
11-0 x 13-0

up

d w

BED RM./ STUDY
11-4 x 12-0
(vaulted ceiling)

PORCH

GARAGE
21-0 x 21-0

BED RM.
13-4 x 11-8

walk-in closet

bath

walk-in closet

sto.

lin.

BED RM.
13-4 x 11-8

attic stor.

attic stor.

foyer below

SECOND FLOOR

PORCH

BRKFST.
10-0 x 10-0

(vaulted ceiling)

MASTER BED RM.
15-4 x 14-4

master bath

KITCHEN
13-8 x 11-8

walk-in closet

UTILITY
7-8 x 6-0

d   w

storage

pan.

pd. rm.

GARAGE
21-0 x 21-0

sto.

DINING
13-8 x 12-8

cl

up

© 2001 DONALD A. GARDNER
All rights reserved

FOYER
7-8 x 7-6

FIRST FLOOR

fireplace

GREAT RM.
16-0 x 19-8

shelves

(vaulted ceiling)

PORCH

plan # HPT910126

- STYLE: COUNTRY COTTAGE
- FIRST FLOOR: 1,608 SQ. FT.
- SECOND FLOOR: 581 SQ. FT.
- TOTAL: 2,189 SQ. FT.
- BEDROOMS: 3
- BATHROOMS: 2½
- WIDTH: 46'-0"
- DEPTH: 63'-0"

SEARCH ONLINE @ EPLANS.COM

Arched lintels and a stone pediment add European flair to this design, while a wide porch support and matchstick detailing add a Craftsman flavor. The expansive great room, just to the left of the foyer, boasts a vaulted ceiling, a fireplace and built-in bookshelves; elegant columns define the adjacent dining room. The kitchen showcases a central island cooktop and opens to a cozy porch. The master suite, conveniently close to the laundry area, also features a vaulted ceiling as well as a walk-in closet. On the second floor, two family bedrooms include walk-in closets and share a full bath.

TO ORDER BLUEPRINTS CALL TOLL FREE 1-800-521-6797

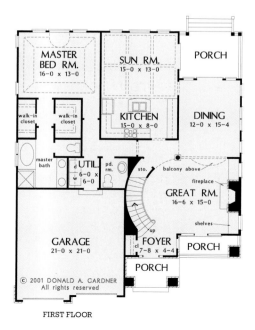

© 2001 Donald A. Gardner, Inc.

plan # HPT910127

- **STYLE: COUNTRY COTTAGE**
- **FIRST FLOOR: 1,542 SQ. FT.**
- **SECOND FLOOR: 752 SQ. FT.**
- **TOTAL: 2,294 SQ. FT.**
- **BONUS SPACE: 370 SQ. FT.**
- **BEDROOMS: 3**
- **BATHROOMS: 2½**
- **WIDTH: 44'-4"**
- **DEPTH: 54'-0"**

SEARCH ONLINE @ EPLANS.COM

A unique mixture of stone, siding, and windows create character in this Arts and Crafts design. Columns, decorative railing and a metal roof add architectural interest to an intimate front porch, while a rock entryway frames a French door flanked by sidelights and crowned with a transom. An elegant, curved staircase highlights the grand two-story foyer and great room. A clerestory floods both the great room and second-floor loft with light. A delightful sun room can be accessed from the dining room and is open to the kitchen. Upstairs, closets act as noise barriers between two bedrooms, and the bonus room can be used as a home theatre or recreation room.

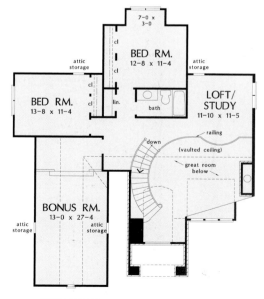

FIRST FLOOR

SECOND FLOOR

CABINS & COTTAGES

© 2001 Donald A. Gardner, Inc.

A trio of dormers, metal porch covering and a mixture of stone and siding create a modern version of the traditional American home. The front porch is bordered by columns and features a trio of arches. A fireplace and built-ins, along with a cathedral ceiling that flows to the kitchen, highlight the great room. Tray ceilings crown the dining room and master bedroom, while visually expanding space. The bonus room makes a perfect playroom for kids, separating the noise from the common living areas and master bedroom. The master bath is complete with a sizable shower, double vanity, garden tub and a private toilet.

plan # HPT910128

- STYLE: COUNTRY COTTAGE
- SQUARE FOOTAGE: 1,674
- BONUS SPACE: 336 SQ. FT.
- BEDROOMS: 3
- BATHROOMS: 2
- WIDTH: 56'-4"
- DEPTH: 50'-0"

SEARCH ONLINE @ EPLANS.COM

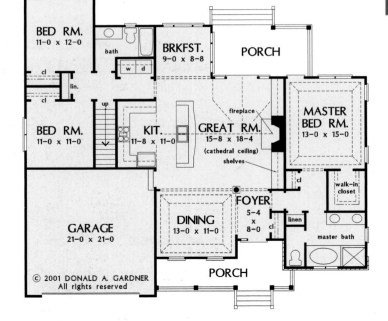

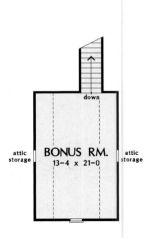

TO ORDER BLUEPRINTS CALL TOLL FREE 1-800-521-6797

eplans.com

THE GATEWAY
TO YOUR NEW HOME

Looking for more plans? Got questions?
Try our one-stop home plans resource—eplans.com.

We'll help you streamline the plan selection process, so your dreams can become reality faster than you ever imagined. From choosing your home plan and ideal location to finding an experienced contractor, eplans.com will guide you every step of the way.

Mix and match! Explore! At eplans.com you can combine all your top criteria to find your perfect match. Search for your ideal home plan by any or all of the following:

> Number of bedrooms or baths
> Total square feet
> House style
> Designer
> Cost

With over 10,000 plans, the options are endless. Colonial, ranch, country, and Victorian are just a few of the house styles offered. Keep in mind your essential lifestyle features—whether to include a porch, fireplace, bonus room, or main floor laundry room. And the garage—how many cars must it accommodate, if any? By filling out the preference page on eplans.com, we'll help you narrow your search. And, don't forget to enjoy a virtual home tour before any decisions are set in stone.

At eplans.com we'll make the building process a snap to understand. At the click of a button you'll find a complete building guide. And our eplan task planner will create a construction calendar just for you. Here you'll find links to tips and other valuable information to help you every step of the way—from choosing a site to moving day.

For your added convenience, our home plans experts are available for live, one-on-one chats at eplans.com. Building a home may seem like a complicated project, but it doesn't have to be—particularly if you'll let us help you from start to finish.

COPYRIGHT DOS & DON'TS

Blueprints for residential construction (or working drawings, as they are often called in the industry) are copyrighted intellectual property, protected under the terms of United States Copyright Law and, therefore, cannot be copied legally for use in building. However, we've made it easy for you to get what you need to build your home, without violating copyright law. Following are some guidelines to help you obtain the right number of copies for your chosen blueprint design.

COPYRIGHT DO

■ Do purchase enough copies of the blueprints to satisfy building requirements. As a rule for a home or project plan, you will need a set for yourself, two or three for your builder and subcontractors, two for the local building department, and one to three for your mortgage lender. You may want to check with your local building department or your builder to see how many they need before you purchase. You may need to buy eight to 10 sets; note that some areas of the country require purchase of vellums (also called reproducibles) instead of blueprints. Vellums can be written on and changed more easily than blueprints. Also, remember, plans are only good for one-time construction.

■ Do consider reverse blueprints if you want to flop the plan. Lettering and numbering will appear backward, but the reversed sets will help you and your builder better visualize the design.

■ Do take advantage of multiple-set discounts at the time you place your order. Usually, purchasing additional sets after you receive your initial order is not as cost-effective.

■ Do take advantage of vellums. Though they are a little more expensive, they can be changed, copied, and used for one-time construction of a home. You will receive a copyright release letter with your vellums that will allow you to have them copied.

■ Do talk with one of our professional service representatives before placing your order. They can give you great advice about what packages are available for your chosen design and what will work best for your particular situation.

COPYRIGHT DON'T

■ Don't think you should purchase only one set of blueprints for a building project. One is fine if you want to study the plan closely, but will not be enough for actual building.

■ Don't expect your builder or a copy center to make copies of standard blueprints. They cannot legally—most copy centers are aware of this.

■ Don't purchase standard blueprints if you know you'll want to make changes to the plans; vellums are a better value.

■ Don't use blueprints or vellums more than one time. Additional fees apply if you want to build more than one time from a set of drawings. ■

LET US SHOW YOU OUR HOME BLUEPRINT PACKAGE.

BUILDING A HOME? PLANNING A HOME?

OUR BLUEPRINT PACKAGE HAS NEARLY EVERYTHING YOU NEED TO GET THE JOB DONE RIGHT,

whether you're working on your own or with help from an architect, designer, builder or subcontractors. Each Blueprint Package is the result of many hours of work by licensed architects or professional designers.

QUALITY

Hundreds of hours of painstaking effort have gone into the development of your blueprint plan. Each home has been quality-checked by professionals to insure accuracy and buildability.

VALUE

Because we sell in volume, you can buy professional quality blueprints at a fraction of their development cost. With our plans, your dream home design costs substantially less than the fees charged by architects.

SERVICE

Once you've chosen your favorite home plan, you'll receive fast, efficient service whether you choose to mail or fax your order to us or call us toll free at 1-800-521-6797. After you have received your order, call for customer service toll free 1-888-690-1116.

SATISFACTION

Over 50 years of service to satisfied home plan buyers provide us unparalleled experience and knowledge in producing quality blueprints.

ORDER TOLL FREE 1-800-521-6797

After you've looked over our Blueprint Package and Important Extras, call toll free on our Blueprint Hotline: 1-800-521-6797, for current pricing and availability prior to mailing the order form on page 191. We're ready and eager to serve you. After you have received your order, call for customer service toll free 1-888-690-1116.

Each set of blueprints is an interrelated collection of detail sheets which includes components such as floor plans, interior and exterior elevations, dimensions, cross-sections, diagrams and notations. These sheets show exactly how your house is to be built.

SETS MAY INCLUDE:

FRONTAL SHEET
This artist's sketch of the exterior of the house gives you an idea of how the house will look when built and landscaped. Large floor plans show all levels of the house and provide an overview of your new home's livability, as well as a handy reference for deciding on furniture placement.

FOUNDATION PLANS
This sheet shows the foundation layout including support walls, excavated and unexcavated areas, if any, and foundation notes. If slab construction rather than basement, the plan shows footings and details for a monolithic slab. This page, or another in the set, may include a sample plot plan for locating your house on a building site.

DETAILED FLOOR PLANS
These plans show the layout of each floor of the house. Rooms and interior spaces are carefully dimensioned and keys are given for cross-section details provided later in the plans. The positions of electrical outlets and switches are shown.

HOUSE CROSS-SECTIONS
Large-scale views show sections or cut-aways of the foundation, interior walls, exterior walls, floors, stairways and roof details. Additional cross-sections may show important changes in floor, ceiling or roof heights or the relationship of one level to another. Extremely valuable for construction, these sections show exactly how the various parts of the house fit together.

INTERIOR ELEVATIONS
Many of our drawings show the design and placement of kitchen and bathroom cabinets, laundry areas, fireplaces, bookcases and other built-ins. Little "extras," such as mantelpiece and wainscoting drawings, plus molding sections, provide details that give your home that custom touch.

EXTERIOR ELEVATIONS
These drawings show the front, rear and sides of your house and give necessary notes on exterior materials and finishes. Particular attention is given to cornice detail, brick and stone accents or other finish items that make your home unique.

IMPORTANT EXTRAS TO DO THE JOB RIGHT!

INTRODUCING IMPORTANT PLANNING AND CONSTRUCTION
AIDS DEVELOPED BY OUR PROFESSIONALS TO HELP YOU
SUCCEED IN YOUR HOME-BUILDING PROJECT

MATERIALS LIST

(Note: Because of the diversity of local building codes, our Materials List does not include mechanical materials.)

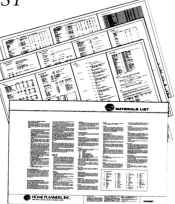

For many of the designs in our portfolio, we offer a customized materials take-off that is invaluable in planning and estimating the cost of your new home. This Materials List outlines the quantity, type and size of materials needed to build your house (with the exception of mechanical system items). Included are framing lumber, windows and doors, kitchen and bath cabinetry, rough and finish hardware, and much more. This handy list helps you or your builder cost out materials and serves as a reference sheet when you're compiling bids. Some Materials Lists may be ordered before blueprints are ordered, call for information.

SPECIFICATION OUTLINE

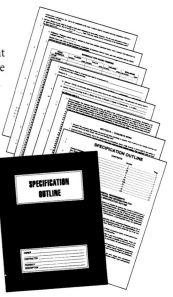

This valuable 16-page document is critical to building your house correctly. Designed to be filled in by you or your builder, this book lists 166 stages or items crucial to the building process. It provides a comprehensive review of the construction process and helps in choosing materials. When combined with the blueprints, a signed contract, and a schedule, it becomes a legal document and record for the building of your home.

QUOTE ONE®

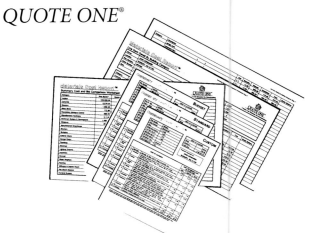

SUMMARY COST REPORT   **MATERIAL COST REPORT**

A product for estimating the cost of building select designs, the Quote One® system is available in two separate stages: The Summary Cost Report and the Material Cost Report.

The **Summary Cost Report** is the first stage in the package and shows the total cost per square foot for your chosen home in your zip-code area and then breaks that cost down into various categories showing the costs for building materials, labor and installation. The report includes three grades: Budget, Standard and Custom. These reports allow you to evaluate your building budget and compare the costs of building a variety of homes in your area.

Make even more informed decisions about your home-building project with the second phase of our package, our **Material Cost Report.** This tool is invaluable in planning and estimating the cost of your new home. The material and installation (labor and equipment) cost is shown for each of over 1,000 line items provided in the Materials List (Standard grade), which is included when you purchase this estimating tool. It allows you to determine building costs for your specific zip-code area and for your chosen home design. Space is allowed for additional estimates from contractors and subcontractors, such as for mechanical materials, which are not included in our packages. This invaluable tool includes a Materials List. A Material Cost Report cannot be ordered before blueprints are ordered. Call for details. In addition, ask about our Home Planners Estimating Package.

If you are interested in a plan that is not indicated as Quote One®, please call and ask our sales reps. They will be happy to verify the status for you. To order these invaluable reports, use the order form.

186 THE DESIGNS OF DONALD A. GARDNER   TO ORDER BLUEPRINTS CALL TOLL FREE 1-800-521-6797

CONSTRUCTION INFORMATION

If you want to know more about techniques— and deal more confidently with subcontractors — we offer these useful sheets. Each set is an excellent tool that will add to your understanding of these technical subjects. These helpful details provide general construction information and are not specific to any single plan.

PLUMBING
The Blueprint Package includes locations for all the plumbing fixtures, including sinks, lavatories, tubs, showers, toilets, laundry trays and water heaters. However, if you want to know more about the complete plumbing system, these Plumbing Details will prove very useful. Prepared to meet requirements of the National Plumbing Code, these fact-filled sheets give general information on pipe schedules, fittings, sump-pump details, water-softener hookups, septic system details and much more. Sheets also include a glossary of terms.

ELECTRICAL
The locations for every electrical switch, plug and outlet are shown in your Blueprint Package. However, these Electrical Details go further to take the mystery out of household electrical systems. Prepared to meet requirements of the National Electrical Code, these comprehensive drawings come packed with helpful information, including wire sizing, switch-installation schematics, cable-routing details, appliance wattage, doorbell hook-ups, typical service panel circuitry and much more. A glossary of terms is also included.

CONSTRUCTION
The Blueprint Package contains information an experienced builder needs to construct a particular house. However, it doesn't show all the ways that houses can be built, nor does it explain alternate construction methods. To help you understand how your house will be built—and offer additional techniques—this set of Construction Details depicts the materials and methods used to build foundations, fireplaces, walls, floors and roofs. Where appropriate, the drawings show acceptable alternatives.

MECHANICAL
These Mechanical Details contain fundamental principles and useful data that will help you make informed decisions and communicate with subcontractors about heating and cooling systems. Drawings contain instructions and samples that allow you to make simple load calculations, and preliminary sizing and costing analysis. Covered are the most commonly used systems from heat pumps to solar fuel systems. The package is filled with illustrations and diagrams to help you visualize components and how they relate to one another.

THE HANDS-ON HOME FURNITURE PLANNER

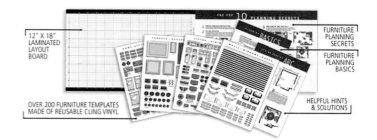

Effectively plan the space in your home using The **Hands-On Home Furniture Planner**. It's fun and easy—no more moving heavy pieces of furniture to see how the room will go together. And you can try different layouts, moving furniture at a whim.

The kit includes reusable peel and stick furniture templates that fit onto a 12" x 18" laminated layout board—space enough to layout every room in your home.

Also included in the package are a number of helpful planning tools. You'll receive:

✓ Helpful hints and solutions for difficult situations.
✓ Furniture planning basics to get you started.
✓ Furniture planning secrets that let you in on some of the tricks of professional designers.

The **Hands-On Home Furniture Planner** is the one tool that no new homeowner or home remodeler should be without. It's also a perfect housewarming gift!

To Order, Call Toll Free
1-800-521-6797

After you've looked over our Blueprint Package and Important Extras on these pages, call for current pricing and availability prior to mailing the order form. We're ready and eager to serve you. After you have received your order, call for customer service toll free 1-888-690-1116.

BLUEPRINT PRICE SCHEDULE

Prices guaranteed through December 31, 2003

TIERS	1-SET STUDY PACKAGE	4-SET BUILDING PACKAGE	8-SET BUILDING PACKAGE	1-SET REPRODUCIBLE*
P1	$20	$50	$90	$140
P2	$40	$70	$110	$160
P3	$70	$100	$140	$190
P4	$100	$130	$170	$220
P5	$140	$170	$210	$270
P6	$180	$210	$250	$310
A1	$440	$480	$520	$660
A2	$480	$520	$560	$720
A3	$530	$575	$615	$800
A4	$575	$620	$660	$870
C1	$620	$665	$710	$935
C2	$670	$715	$760	$1000
C3	$715	$760	$805	$1075
C4	$765	$810	$855	$1150
L1	$870	$925	$975	$1300
L2	$945	$1000	$1050	$1420
L3	$1050	$1105	$1155	$1575
L4	$1155	$1210	$1260	$1735
SQ1				.35/sq. ft.

* Requires a fax number

OPTIONS FOR PLANS IN TIERS A1–L4

Additional Identical Blueprints
in same order for "A1–L4" price plans ....$50 per set
Reverse Blueprints (mirror image)
with 4- or 8-set order for "A1–L4" plans ....$50 fee per order
Specification Outlines ....$10 each
Materials Lists for "A1–C3" plans ....$60 each
Materials Lists for "C4–SQ1" plans ....$70 each

OPTIONS FOR PLANS IN TIERS P1–P6

Additional Identical Blueprints
in same order for "P1–P6" price plans ....$10 per set
Reverse Blueprints (mirror image) for "P1–P6" price plans ....$10 fee per order
1 Set of Deck Construction Details...$14.95 each
Deck Construction Package ....add $10 to Building Package price
*(includes 1 set of "P1–P6" plans, plus
1 set Standard Deck Construction Details)*

IMPORTANT NOTES

- SQ one-set building package includes one set of reproducible vellum construction drawings plus one set of study blueprints.
- The 1-set study package is marked "not for construction."
- Prices for 4- or 8-set Building Packages honored only at time of original order.
- Some foundations carry a $225 surcharge.
- Right-reading reverse blueprints, if available, will incur a $165 surcharge.
- Additional identical blueprints may be purchased within 60 days of original order.

TO USE THE INDEX,

refer to the design number listed in numerical order (a helpful page reference is also given). Note the price tier and refer to the Blueprint Price Schedule above for the cost of one, four or eight sets of blueprints or the cost of a reproducible drawing. Additional prices are shown for identical and reverse blueprint sets, as well as a very useful Materials List for some of the plans. Also note in the Plan Index those plans that have Deck Plans or Landscape Plans. Refer to the schedules above for prices of these plans. The letter "Y" identifies plans that are part of our Quote One® estimating service and those that offer Materials Lists.

TO ORDER,

Call toll free 1-800-521-6797 for current pricing and availability prior to mailing the order form. FAX: 1-800-224-6699 or 520-544-3086.

PLAN INDEX

DESIGN	PRICE	PAGE	MATERIALS LIST	QUOTE ONE®
HPT910001	C2	16	Y	
HPT910002	C1	12	Y	
HPT910003	SQ1	44		
HPT910004	C1	29	Y	
HPT910005	C2	21	Y	
HPT910006	A4	34	Y	Y
HPT910007	C2	38	Y	
HPT910008	C2	8	Y	
HPT910009	A4	26	Y	
HPT910010	C3	50	Y	
HPT910011	C3	52	Y	
HPT910012	A4	54	Y	
HPT910013	A4	56	Y	Y
HPT910014	A4	58	Y	
HPT910015	C1	59	Y	
HPT910016	C1	60	Y	

BEFORE FILLING OUT THE ORDER FORM, PLEASE CALL US ON OUR TOLL-FREE BLUEPRINT HOTLINE 1-800-521-6797. YOU MAY WANT TO LEARN MORE ABOUT OUR SERVICES AND PRODUCTS. HERE'S SOME INFORMATION YOU WILL FIND HELPFUL.

OUR EXCHANGE POLICY

With the exception of reproducible plan orders, we will exchange your entire first order for an equal or greater number of blueprints within our plan collection within 90 days of the original order. The entire content of your original order must be returned before an exchange will be processed. Please call our customer service department for your return authorization number and shipping instructions. If the returned blueprints look used, redlined or copied, we will not honor your exchange. Fees for exchanging your blueprints are as follows: 20% of the amount of the original order...plus the difference in cost if exchanging for a design in a higher price bracket or less the difference in cost if exchanging for a design in a lower price bracket. (**Reproducible blueprints are not exchangeable or refundable.**) Please call for current postage and handling prices. Shipping and handling charges are not refundable.

ABOUT REPRODUCIBLES

When purchasing a reproducible you may be required to furnish a fax number. The designer will fax documents that you must sign and return to them before shipping will take place.

ABOUT REVERSE BLUEPRINTS

Although lettering and dimensions will appear backward, reverses will be a useful aid if you decide to flop the plan. See Price Schedule and Plans Index for pricing.

REVISING, MODIFYING AND CUSTOMIZING PLANS

Like many homeowners who buy these plans, you and your builder, architect or engineer may want to make changes to them. We recommend purchase of a reproducible plan for any changes made by your builder, licensed architect or engineer. As set forth below, we cannot assume any responsibility for blueprints which have been changed, whether by you, your builder or by professionals selected by you or referred to you by us, because such individuals are outside our supervision and control.

ARCHITECTURAL AND ENGINEERING SEALS

Some cities and states are now requiring that a licensed architect or engineer review and "seal" a blueprint, or officially approve it, prior to construction due to concerns over energy costs, safety and other factors. Prior to application for a building permit or the start of actual construction, we strongly advise that you consult your local building official who can tell you if such a review is required.

ABOUT THE DESIGNS

The architects and designers whose work appears in this publication are among America's leading residential designers. Each plan was designed to meet the requirements of a nationally recognized model building code in effect at the time and place the plan was drawn. Because national building codes change from time to time, plans may not comply with any such code at the time they are sold to a customer. In addition, building officials may not accept these plans as final construction documents of record as the plans may need to be modified and additional drawings and details added to suit local conditions and requirements. We strongly advise that purchasers consult a licensed architect or engineer, and their local building official, before starting any construction related to these plans.

LOCAL BUILDING CODES AND ZONING REQUIREMENTS

At the time of creation, our plans are drawn to specifications published by the Building Officials and Code Administrators (BOCA) International, Inc.; the Southern Building Code Congress (SBCCI) International, Inc.; the International Conference of Building Officials (ICBO); or the Council of American Building Officials (CABO). Our plans are designed to meet or exceed national building standards. Because of the great differences in geography and climate throughout the United States and Canada, each state, county and municipality has its own building codes, zone requirements, ordinances and building regulations. Your plan may need to be modified to comply with local requirements regarding snow loads, energy codes, soil and seismic conditions and a wide range of other matters. In addition, you may need to obtain permits or inspections from local governments before and in the course of construction. Prior to using blueprints ordered from us, we strongly advise that you consult a licensed architect or engineer—and speak with your local building official—before applying for any permit or beginning construction. We authorize the use of our blueprints on the express condition that you strictly comply with all local building codes, zoning requirements and other applicable laws, regulations, ordinances and requirements. Notice: Plans for homes to be built in Nevada must be re-drawn by a Nevada-registered professional. Consult your building official for more information on this subject.

TOLL FREE
1-800-521-6797

REGULAR OFFICE HOURS:
8:00 a.m.-9:00 p.m. EST, Monday-Friday

If we receive your order by 3:00 p.m. EST, Monday-Friday, we'll process it and ship within **two business days**. When ordering by phone, please have your credit card or check information ready. We'll also ask you for the Order Form Key Number at the bottom of the order form.

By FAX: Copy the Order Form on the next page and send it on our FAX line: 1-800-224-6699 or 520-544-3086.

Canadian Customers
Order Toll Free 1-877-223-6389

ORDER FORM

CALL FOR CURRENT PRICING & AVAILABILITY PRIOR TO MAILING THIS ORDER FORM.

DISCLAIMER

The designers we work with have put substantial care and effort into the creation of their blueprints. However, because they cannot provide on-site consultation, supervision and control over actual construction, and because of the great variance in local building requirements, building practices and soil, seismic, weather and other conditions, WE CANNOT MAKE ANY WARRANTY, EXPRESS OR IMPLIED, WITH RESPECT TO THE CONTENT OR USE OF THE BLUEPRINTS, INCLUDING BUT NOT LIMITED TO ANY WARRANTY OF MERCHANTABILITY OR OF FITNESS FOR A PARTICULAR PURPOSE. ITEMS, PRICES, TERMS AND CONDITIONS ARE SUBJECT TO CHANGE WITHOUT NOTICE. REPRODUCIBLE PLAN ORDERS MAY REQUIRE A CUSTOMER'S SIGNED RELEASE BEFORE SHIPPING.

TERMS AND CONDITIONS

These designs are protected under the terms of United States Copyright Law and may not be copied or reproduced in any way, by any means, unless you have purchased Reproducibles which clearly indicate your right to copy or reproduce. We authorize the use of your chosen design as an aid in the construction of one single family home only. You may not use this design to build a second or multiple dwellings without purchasing another blueprint or blueprints or paying additional design fees.

HOW MANY BLUEPRINTS DO YOU NEED?

Although a standard building package may satisfy many states, cities and counties, some plans may require certain changes. For your convenience, we have developed a Reproducible plan which allows a local professional to modify and make up to 10 copies of your revised plan. As our plans are all copyright protected, with your purchase of the Reproducible, we will supply you with a Copyright release letter. The number of copies you may need: 1 for owner; 3 for builder; 2 for local building department and 1-3 sets for your mortgage lender.

☎ ORDER TOLL FREE!

For information about any of our services or to order call 1-800-521-6797

Browse our website: www.eplans.com

BLUEPRINTS ARE NOT REFUNDABLE EXCHANGES ONLY

For Customer Service, call toll free 1-888-690-1116.

HOME PLANNERS, LLC wholly owned by Hanley-Wood, LLC
3275 WEST INA ROAD, SUITE 220 • TUCSON, ARIZONA • 85741

THE BASIC BLUEPRINT PACKAGE
Rush me the following (please refer to the Plans Index and Price Schedule in this section):
____ Set(s) of reproducibles*, plan number(s) _____ $_____
    indicate foundation type _____ surcharge (if applicable): $_____
____ Set(s) of blueprints, plan number(s) _____ indicate foundation type _____ $_____
    indicate foundation type _____ surcharge (if applicable): $_____
____ Additional identical blueprints (standard or reverse) in same order @ $50 per set $_____
____ Reverse blueprints @ $50 fee per order. Right-reading reverse @ $165 surcharge $_____

IMPORTANT EXTRAS
Rush me the following:
____ Materials List: $60 (Must be purchased with Blueprint set.) Add $10 for Schedule C4–SQ1 plans $_____
____ **Quote One®** Summary Cost Report @ $29.95 for one, $14.95 for each additional,
    for plans _____ $_____
    Building location: City _____ Zip Code _____
____ **Quote One®** Material Cost Report @ $120 Schedules P1–C3; $130 Schedules C4–SQ1,
    for plan _____ (Must be purchased with Blueprints set.) $_____
    Building location: City _____ Zip Code _____
____ Specification Outlines @ $10 each $_____
____ Detail Sets @ $14.95 each; any two $22.95; any three $29.95; all four for $39.95 (save $19.85) $_____
    ❏ Plumbing ❏ Electrical ❏ Construction ❏ Mechanical
____ Home Furniture Planner @ $15.95 each $_____

DECK BLUEPRINTS
(Please refer to the Plans Index and Price Schedule in this section)
____ Set(s) of Deck Plan _____ $_____
____ Additional identical blueprints in same order @ $10 per set. $_____
____ Reverse blueprints @ $10 fee per order. $_____
____ Set of Standard Deck Details @ $14.95 per set. $_____
____ Set of Complete Deck Construction Package (Best Buy!) Add $10 to Building Package.
    Includes Custom Deck Plan _____ Plus Standard Deck Details

LANDSCAPE BLUEPRINTS
(Please refer to the Plans Index and Price Schedule in this section.)
____ Set(s) of Landscape Plan _____ $_____
____ Additional identical blueprints in same order @ $10 per set $_____
____ Reverse blueprints @ $10 fee per order $_____
Please indicate appropriate region of the country for Plant & Material List. Region _____

POSTAGE AND HANDLING *SIGNATURE IS REQUIRED FOR ALL DELIVERIES.*	1–3 sets	4+ sets
DELIVERY No CODs (Requires street address—No P.O. Boxes)		
•Regular Service (Allow 7–10 business days delivery)	❏ $20.00	❏ $25.00
•Priority (Allow 4–5 business days delivery)	❏ $25.00	❏ $35.00
•Express (Allow 3 business days delivery)	❏ $35.00	❏ $45.00
OVERSEAS DELIVERY	fax, phone or mail for quote	

Note: All delivery times are from date Blueprint Package is shipped.

POSTAGE (From box above) $_____
SUBTOTAL $_____
SALES TAX (AZ & MI residents, please add appropriate state and local sales tax.) $_____
TOTAL (Subtotal and tax) $_____

YOUR ADDRESS (please print legibly)

Name _____

Street _____

City_____ State _____ Zip_____

Daytime telephone number (required) (_____) _____

* Fax number (required for reproducible orders) _____
TeleCheck® Checks By Phone℠ available

FOR CREDIT CARD ORDERS ONLY

Credit card number _____ Exp. Date: (M/Y) _____
Check one ❏ Visa ❏ MasterCard ❏ American Express

Order Form Key
HPT91

Signature (required)_____
Please check appropriate box: ❏ Licensed Builder-Contractor ❏ Homeowner

 **ORDER TOLL FREE!**
1-800-521-6797

BY FAX: Copy the order form above and send it on our FAXLINE: 1-800-224-6699 OR 520-544-3086

A rustic stone fireplace, a hardwood floor, and soothing shades of blue establish the country character of this room. To view the floor plans, see page 50.